# THE
# GREATEST
# NOBODIES
# *of* HISTORY

# THE GREATEST NOBODIES of HISTORY

*Minor Characters*
*from Major Moments*

## ADRIAN BLISS

BALLANTINE BOOKS

NEW YORK

Published in the United States by Ballantine Books, an imprint of Random House, a division of Penguin Random House LLC, New York.

BALLANTINE BOOKS & colophon are registered trademarks of Penguin Random House LLC.

Originally published in the United Kingdom by Century, Penguin Group UK, a Penguin Random House company.

Hardback ISBN 978-0-593-97716-3
Ebook ISBN 978-0-593-98240-2

Printed in the United States of America on acid-free paper

randomhousebooks.com

1st Printing

First Edition

*For the nobodies*

# Contents

# Author's Note

I think it was Julius Caesar's barber who once said, "Everyone remembers the heroes, but it is the nobodies who make history," which was just *so* like him. He was right, of course. If Genghis Khan's childhood nanny had been a touch more attentive, and if Alexander the Great's friends hadn't suggested a group trip to Persia, everything would've been different. Neither you nor I would be here and this book would never have been published. Thankfully, in this timeline, everyone did their bit, from Michelangelo's marble dealer to Cleopatra's hairstylist and as such, we are all here, and so is this book.

The following pages contain the (mostly) true stories of ten extraordinary side characters from humanity's biggest moments. Some historians will discredit my sources. They'll tell you there's just no way a psychic medium contacted a ferret and transcribed its memoir, or that a nineteenth-century horse could be so articulate. To these naysayers, I say this: it is impossible for us to know exactly how any historical event unfolded. The past is overflowing with embellished tales, subtle propaganda, outright lies, vicious rumors, harmless exaggerations, misheard anecdotes and people just getting things wrong. In history, nothing is certain, so perhaps, and just perhaps, the lives of its greatest nobodies went a little something like this . . .

# THE GREATEST NOBODIES *of* HISTORY

I.

# The Dog Philosopher

In the fourth century BCE, under the watchful eye of Zeus and the Olympians, Ancient Athens and its mortals were enjoying the fruits of the golden age. After a hundred years of good fortune, the marble city gleamed with temples to the gods and heroes, and its people (or at least the lucky ones) enjoyed a life of enlightenment, strolling about on the cobbles, thinking up inspirational quotes.

The most famous of these thinkers—Socrates, Plato and Aristotle—fascinated, dazzled and discombobulated their fellow Athenians with their philosophies, eventually making a cultural impact so large they are still household names to this day. Unfairly, their equally fascinating contemporary, the cynical Diogenes of Sinope, isn't quite as well known, most of his life and teachings being lost to time.

That all changed in 2009, however, when a hoard of letters was found buried under the Ancient Agora of Athens. After spending more than a decade translating the documents and filtering out the junk mail, historians were able to piece together an extraordinary collection of complaint letters from a disgruntled Athenian citizen, finally shedding light on the controversial antics of the man Plato dubbed "Socrates gone mad."

---

To whom it may concern,

I am writing to file an official complaint regarding a disturbance in my neighborhood.

I should caveat that I am a very kind and tolerant man. Sometimes my friends say I am too kind and too tolerant, and that I need to stop being so kind and tolerant, but I'm afraid it is in my nature and not subject to change.

This morning, while leaving my home on Aphrodite Avenue, I found that my route past the Temple of Apollo* was blocked by a very large, overturned stone jar. Passersby agreed it was a dreadful shame, for it is a beautiful street in an upmarket part of town, and to see it go to the dogs in this way was most upsetting.

I was already running late to brunch with my mother, but as an honorable citizen it felt remiss not to stop and investigate. Well, I wish I hadn't, for as I drew closer I was hit by the most heinous stench which remains in my nostrils still!

"Whose pithos is this?" I said, covering my nose with my chiton. I looked around for the offender. "Who has left a

---

*The Temple of Apollo Patroos situated in the Ancient Agora of Athens. The Agora was the beating heart of Athenian life, and by extension the bedrock of Western civilization. Here the city's citizens would meet to conduct business, attend a political gathering, worship at a sacred temple, purchase a little something at a shop or stall, and occasionally cower for their lives while Persians, Romans or Vikings ransacked the place.

giant jar of feces and carcasses in the middle of the street?"
A boy sitting on the steps of the temple stared blankly and
shrugged. No one owned up.

I was bending down to look inside when, to my horror, it
moved. I jumped back, and from the cavity came a man,
unfolding his arms and legs until he was outstretched and
yawning, completely naked. All the flies in Athens seemed to
gather, drinking up the cloud of noxious gas that encircled
him.

"You can't leave your pithos here!" I stuttered. The man
rubbed his eyes and scratched his groin.

"It's not my pithos," he said, before stumbling over to the
temple and relieving himself against one of its columns. "It's
nobody's."

I left, trying to process what I had just seen, and by the
time I arrived at brunch (ten minutes late), the smell of sweat
and urine still hadn't left me, making it very difficult to enjoy
my English yogurt.

Now, before you make assumptions, I should tell you that
I am a big—no, *huge*—advocate of poor people. Just last week
I smiled at a homeless orphan in the Agora and I even have
that thing Plato said, "Be kind, for everyone you meet is
fighting a harder battle," on a tote bag. But it works both
ways! I'm still putting off taking a wife (purely for financial
reasons, there are plenty of women who like me) and I've just
had to sell my second home on Aegina. Times are tight, but
we must keep up appearances. We must rise above the
barbarous domain of animals and live ordered, civilized lives.
Otherwise, we are merely dogs!

On behalf of all the good people of Athens, I request the
man be moved to a more suitable neighborhood. It breaks

my heart to see him look so out of place, and I can't help but feel he would be much happier living in one of those lovely far-off suburbs.

I look forward to your swift action in this matter.

Yours sincerely,
Concerned Citizen of Athens
No. 24 Aphrodite Avenue
Kerameikos district
Athens

P.S. Thank you for *finally* removing the illegally deposited cone on the statue of Eros.

*

To whom it may concern,

Just following up on my previous letter. Did you receive it? Only, it has been three days and the unsavory man seems to have set up permanent camp next to the Temple of Apollo. Thankfully he now wears a chiton from time to time, but his odor still offends everyone within a four-mile radius. Has he not heard of Aesop?

In case you're of the opinion that desecrating a holy temple and spoiling its aesthetics isn't grounds for exile, I would like to tell you about what happened today in the marketplace.

Now, I don't normally visit the marketplace (I have slaves to do that for me) but my 30th birthday is coming up and I intend to put on a fabulous party for my many friends, acquaintances and prospective business clients. There has never been a more perfect opportunity to show them all just what kind of man I am, so I am going all out.

There I was, perusing the fine silks for my birthday chiton, when I heard a ruckus over by the meat and cheese section. The smell alone should've been a giveaway, but I found myself compelled to find out what all the fuss was about.

Lo and behold, there he was, standing in the middle of the aisle munching on a ham and cheese toastie. A circle of mortified onlookers had formed around him, all totally perplexed as to how someone could defy social conventions and *eat in public* like some kind of stray dog.* *This* dog loved the attention and remained on a constant 360-degree rotation so everyone could see his barbaric jaw masticating away.

"You monster!" said a woman, close to tears. The Dog (for if he insists on behaving like a dog I shall call him one) licked his fingers and said, through a mulch of saliva and feta, "If a thing is not shameful in private, why should it be shameful in public?"

I tell you, my eyes rolled so far back into my head they nearly detached. He thinks he's a philosopher! Well, I've never heard anything so hilarious in all my life. Oh how I laughed! I suppose he'll be setting up a school next? I wonder how they'll all fit in his pithos?

Now, I'm an easy-going guy. Childish stunts don't rattle

---

*After witnessing his peculiar antics, the scandalized residents of Athens did indeed call Diogenes a "kyon," or dog. While it was meant as an insult, Diogenes and his followers considered it a badge of honor. After all, dogs lead happy lives, free from the distractions of wealth and the bizarre cultural norms that cripple human beings, like it being obscene to eat in public for some reason.

me. The problem is when these things catch on, which is exactly what happened next.

One of the bewitched onlookers, a well-to-do woman from a respectable family, reached nervously into her pocket, pulled out an almond and started giggling. Before I knew it, she'd popped it in her mouth. Right there in the open! I stared at her, hardly able to believe what I was seeing. She ate another one and another one, grinning the whole time like it was some great thrill. I had to sit down for fear of fainting.

I implore you, for the safety and sanity of all Athenians, to take action before the Dog's horrid ways infect more suggestible civilians. I have seen it happen before! My barber went to ONE Plato lecture and now he's convinced he's a featherless chicken called Paul.* His wife keeps finding him squashed in the coop, harassing the hens. It has completely torn their family apart!

Perhaps you could put the Dog in a little boat and push him out to sea? Alternatively, I've heard the steps of the Acropolis are quite slippery this time of year . . .

Yours impatiently,
Shocked Citizen of Athens
No. 24 Aphrodite Avenue
Kerameikos district
Athens

---

*While trying to settle the age-old debate of "What is a man?," Plato gave the seemingly reasonable response that a man is a featherless animal that walks on two legs. Diogenes, ever the master of debate, countered this by plucking a chicken, throwing its carcass into Plato's Academy and screaming, "Behold! I've brought you a man!" It's fair to say, Plato didn't love the guy.

P.S. Those new marble benches around the Agora are in all the wrong places. Too cold in the morning shade and too hot in the midday sun! Who arranged them, Oedipus?!

★

To whom it may concern,

Hello! Is this thing on? I have yet to receive a response to my two previous letters, both of which are relating to a very serious, very pressing matter.

My 30th birthday is fast approaching and I'll be damned if it's not perfect. The Oracle of Delphi's assistant (the oracle was out) told me it would be a make-or-break occasion, changing the course of my life forever. If that doesn't mean an invite onto the top table of Athens then I don't know what does!

Of course, the bane of my life, the Dog (he's started calling himself that now, like it's a good thing! Can you believe it?) seems determined to scupper my plans. He has moved his pithos from outside the Temple of Apollo to—yes, you guessed it—my front gate! When I asked him why he had moved he told me the pithos rolled down the hill in the night and landed here. Likely story!

Now, I am aware there is no specific law against living in a pithos outside somebody's house, but surely there has to be a law against what happened next.

I was enjoying a private moment alone in my bedroom when I was interrupted by a rabble gathering outside. I put on my chiton and went to have a look, expecting to find the Dog up to one of his usual tricks, but nothing could've prepared me for what I saw.

There he was, sat atop his pithos, chiton over his head, shaking the pillar of the Parthenon for all to see! And by shaking the pillar of the Parthenon I mean clutching his column, strangling his Spartan, man-handling his King Philip of Macedon!* I immediately threw up in my mouth, but like everyone else I couldn't bring myself to look away. A wave of laughter went through the crowd, people no doubt being utterly mystified as to how to react. But cutting through the laughter was the sound of children crying. An unfortunate school group was passing by on their way to the petting zoo.

Grunts in increasing frequency signaled the end of the monstrous performance so I bolted for my front door. Sadly, I didn't quite make it. The schoolteachers covered as many young eyes as possible, but they couldn't save everyone.

"If only it were so easy to soothe a hungry stomach!" said the Dog, bowing and climbing back into his pithos. There was a smattering of unconscionable applause as the onlookers disbanded, leaving me stuck with the horrible little creature installed by my front gate.

Look, we've all done a few evening classes or had a friend drag us along to some old bore's philosophy school. I think we all know what this amateur is trying to say with these outlandish performances, don't we? It doesn't take a genius. If anything, I think he's being too obvious! I got it straight away.

---

*Other sources have testified to this outrageous behavior. In *Lives of the Eminent Philosophers*, written in around the third century CE by Diogenes Laetius (no relation), our pithos dweller was said to regularly fart, spit, urinate and masturbate in public. Those who took issue with this behavior would face him farting, spitting or urinating on *them* (thankfully he stopped there). Eventually Athenians figured out it was easier to simply avoid standing downwind of him.

What happened to nuance? What happened to handing out a pamphlet and going on your way? You would never have caught Socrates with his knob out!* (Except for that one time but I do honestly believe he slipped.)

Please won't you do something about this pseudo-philosopher defecating on the good name of Athens? He is an embarrassment to us all! And he is literally defecating all over Athens! Can't you just tie a weight to his leg and drop him in the Aegean? He would make a nice snack for the fish (if they can stomach the smell).

Yours with mounting fury,
Appalled Citizen of Athens
No. 24 Aphrodite Avenue
Kerameikos district
Athens

P.S. Did you change bin day again? Why have my bins not been collected?

★

Dear Citizen of Athens,

We apologize for the tardy response to your complaints. An administrative error meant your letters were getting redirected to Catering who filed them under "Figure out later."

We have investigated your grievances and were able to speak to the gentleman in question. His name is Diogenes of

---

*By all accounts, Socrates was also a fairly unsavory character and was lacking when it came to personal hygiene. But, credit where it's due, he did stop short of having "me time" in the middle of the high street.

Sinope, and when we broached your complaint with him, he simply said, "Of what use is a philosopher who doesn't hurt anybody's feelings?" And aside from the stench we found him to be an affable man with an interesting outlook on life. We invited him back to the office and he ended up staying all afternoon, fascinating the staff here with his philosophies and anecdotes. We even booked him to do an after-dinner speech at our upcoming summer social.

In regards to your complaint, we gave Diogenes some vouchers for the local baths and have told him about Aesop. He has generously agreed to give himself a little scrub before your 30th birthday celebrations next week.

Kind regards,
Whom it may concern
Council office
The Agora
Athens

*How am I doing? If you're unhappy with the service you received today, please contact the jurors of Athens who will duly ostracize me from the city and send me to my certain death.*

★

To whom it may concern,

Thank you for *finally* responding but I must urge you to reconsider your position. Things have got worse since my last letter, much worse!

In the interest of creating an aspirational environment

for my many friends, acquaintances and prospective business clients, I spent a very large sum of money acquiring luxury rugs, vases, sculptures and artwork to decorate my home. As the slaves accepted the enormous delivery and carried everything inside, I was enjoying educating the admiring crowd on the items I had chosen. There was frivolity in the air and we were all having a pleasurable time when the Dog (still unbathed) climbed on top of his pithos and loudly proclaimed: "He who has the most is content with the least!"

At first people laughed at him, as they should, but then to my horror they started asking questions. "What do you mean?" asked one curious passerby.

"This man," said the Dog, pointing at me, "believes his pretty vases and fine rugs will bring him happiness. He believes they will elevate his position, impress his friends, bring him esteem. All in the search of contentment. This man"—he looked right into my eyes, and all his hypnotized gaggle did the same—"is a fool."

All was silent as half of Athens stood and stared. Even the slaves carrying my things had stopped to listen. I was dumbstruck! Gobsmacked! Speechless! Never have I been so humiliated! I made my excuses and ran inside, reeling from the vicious attack.

How dare the Dog lecture me? ME! I am a respectable man! I live in a house, whereas he lives in a big jar. I wear nice clothes and he wears an old sack (if you're lucky!). He represents the lowest rung of humanity, whereas I represent the highest. I am better than him! How much clearer could it be?

Well, the joke's on him because I have put in an order for even MORE nice things. We all know true happiness can only be achieved through external means. Why else do you think the King of Persia is surrounded by all that gold?

Mark my words, if you let this man ruin my birthday there will be hell to pay!

Yours incandescently,
Incandescent Citizen of Athens
No. 24 Aphrodite Avenue
Kerameikos district
Athens

P.S. The noise coming from the blacksmith's has got *much* louder recently. Has he changed his tools? Please can you have a word.

★

Dear Incandescent Citizen of Athens,

Thank you for your recent letter. We are sorry to hear of your ordeal but must remind you that it is not against the law to do philosophy outside somebody's house. The citizens of Athens are welcome to do philosophy wherever they please, except at the swimming pool.

We advise you to settle this matter with Diogenes directly. Perhaps buy him lunch and ask him to go a bit easier on you?

If someone tries to philosophize you at the swimming pool, please get in touch as a matter of urgency, but until then we're afraid there is not much we can do to help.

We wish you all the best for your upcoming birthday.

Kind regards,
Whom it may concern
Council office
The Agora
Athens


*


To whom it may concern,

Who am I talking to here? Are you the manager? If you're not the manager, then get me the manager!

The Dog's actions are *really* derailing my birthday week. Surely that is a crime? One shouldn't be able to go around derailing other people's birthday weeks unprovoked!

The violent attack on my character has left me unusually pensive. It is not a feeling I am familiar with and not something I particularly like. Here I am, surrounded by nice things but unable to enjoy them. What a waste! And it's all because of the Dog. I fear he is being allowed to run amok in the city, infecting people's minds like an insidious plague.

This morning, while going to fetch my custom birthday chiton from the tailors, I ran into an old acquaintance, a highly intelligent and well-stationed gentleman you no doubt know, Theodoros of Poros (he owns a whole swath of land south of the city). We were exchanging pleasantries when I noticed he wasn't wearing any sandals. I looked at his grazed and dusty feet, stunned, and he said to me, "Oh, that. I'm doing Sandal-less Saturdays."

It had the whiff of the Dog, so I asked him where he had got such an idea.

"My friends and I are really into this new philosopher, Diogenes of Sinope. Have you heard of him? I've been to all his gigs. I think he's just fantastic," he said. I stood there dumbfounded.

"Oh, nice," I managed to stutter, not wanting to fall out of favor with my now mentally compromised old acquaintance.

"Yeah, his whole thing's like radical simplicity and authenticity, y'know? He believes we should reject societal conventions and live more in accordance with nature."*

"Oh cool, I'll check him out," I lied, slipping away. Sandal-less Saturdays! Can you believe it? What's next, tunic-free Tuesdays?! Are we all to stroll about butt naked like animals?

Admittedly, on the way home I tripped over while trying to avoid some feces on the road (wonder where that came from?) and snapped the strap on both of my sandals. Despite trying my best to mend them, I had to walk home barefoot. Yes, it was the most comfortable I've been in years and my backache suddenly disappeared, but was it worth the crippling embarrassment? Absolutely not! I shall be carrying a second pair at all times so my soles never have to touch the earth again.

I fear Theodoros of Poros is too far gone, but something must be done to protect the rest of us from the Dog's philosophical warfare!

Please do not hesitate. Escalate this case to the highest

---

*In rejecting conventional desires for wealth, power and worldly possessions, the removal of footwear is seen as a significant step. Diogenes consistently went barefoot, even in the snow.

level! Who's in charge in this place anyway? It's times like this we need a king. This democracy thing isn't working out. A king wouldn't stand for this nonsense.

Yours despairingly,
Despairing Citizen of Athens
No. 24 Aphrodite Avenue
Kerameikos district
Athens

P.S. I am NOT happy about the proposed road closures for the Panathenaic Games! Please find my much better plan on the enclosed map.

★

Dear Despairing Citizen of Athens,

Sorry, only just seen this! We all slept rough under the stars earlier this week for "Moonlit Mondays" (it's a new weekly event Diogenes is doing up at the Acropolis) and it has had a knock-on effect on our workflow. In addition, Susan, who sorts through our letters and forwards them to the relevant departments, has left the city to live in a cave by the sea.

You'll be pleased to hear we have escalated your case to the highest level and have passed all your letters onto our Area Manager. However, please be aware he is currently doing "Feral Friday" and is sacking off work to forage for berries in the woods.

It has been a pleasure working on your case and we wish you all the best in finding a solution to your grievance.

Kind regards,
Whom it may concern
Council office
The Agora
Athens

*

To whom it may concern,

I should've transcended to the higher echelon today. It was my 30th birthday party, my chance to impress my many friends, acquaintances and prospective business clients and be invited to one of those fancy dinners up on the Acropolis. I poured everything into making this party a resounding success but it has all been for nothing.

When I woke up this morning and tucked into my birthday breakfast, I was determined to keep the Dog out of my mind so I could enjoy the day. I like to stay busy, so I spent a pleasant few hours supervising my slave while he polished the shiny things in my house and later walked through the Agora in my special birthday chiton so anyone not coming to my party could enjoy it too.

As I returned home, I realized I hadn't seen, smelled or even thought of the Dog once all morning, and I felt optimistic about the day ahead. But as soon as the first guests arrived it was clear his pernicious tendrils were everywhere.

They arrived barefoot. Barefoot! To my party! I chastised them and reminded them it wasn't even Saturday. "We're doing this full time now," one of them said. "It just feels right." I couldn't believe my ears when the other barefooters woofed—yes, WOOFED—in assent.

As more guests trickled in (it was a disappointing turnout despite EVERYONE saying they would come), I waited eagerly for their compliments on the decor, on my art and on my special birthday chiton. But, to my horror, no one was impressed by my nice things, despite me choosing the very nicest things from the catalogue. At one point I overheard Theodoros of Poros (who was wearing nothing but a linen sash around his crotch) bitching about my vase collection and calling my painting of a cat with a mustache tacky and embarrassing.

All the usual chatter of such events was replaced by talk of philosophy. More specifically the "philosophy" of the hottest new thinker in town. And to add insult to injury, they all left early to catch the start of his gig on the Acropolis. Even my own mother cut and ran!

I was so upset I crawled into the giant vase I'd purchased for the party and cried myself to sleep, shielded from the cruel world and everyone in it.

Yours crying myself to sleep,
Bereft Citizen of Athens
No. 24 Aphrodite Avenue
Kerameikos district
Athens

P.S. Why is it so surprisingly comfortable to sleep in a vase? It makes absolutely no sense. Do something!

★

Dear Bereft Citizen of Athens,

We are currently out of office for "No-work November" but will endeavor to respond to your letter as soon as we return.

Kind regards,
Whom it may concern
Council office
The Agora
Athens

★

To whom it may concern,

Don't bother. It doesn't matter. You're too late. You stood back and did nothing while an exemplary citizen's good name was torn to shreds.

The party that was meant to change my life has ruined me, and now not even my nice things can bring me solace. As such, I've decided to renounce it all, even my slaves. I dread to think what the poor things will do without me, adrift in the world without a purpose. At least I know how they feel.

I shall be taking a sabbatical to the coast to be sad. Perhaps, someday, I will be able to make sense of this irrational destruction and return to pick up the pieces. Or perhaps I will just tie a weight to my leg and sink into the Aegean.

Either way, you shall not be hearing from me again.

Yours dismantled,
The Shell of a Citizen of Athens
No. 24 Aphrodite Avenue

Kerameikos district
Athens

P.S. Thanks for nothing.

★

Dear Shell,

Apologies for the delay in responding to your letter. We have been working through a lengthy backlog since returning from "No-work November" and since half our team now live in caves by the sea, we are a bit thin on the ground.

We trust your issue has been resolved. Please let us know if this is not the case, otherwise we will go ahead and close your file.

Kind regards,
Whom it may concern
Council office
The Agora
Athens

★

Dear Citizen of Athens,

Since we have not heard from you we have decided to mark your case as resolved. It will now be closed and archived.

Thank you for your continued interest in the safety and well-being of the people of Athens.

Kind regards,
Whom it may concern
Council office
The Agora
Athens

★

To whom it may concern,

I would like to file a complaint about the cobbles outside the Temple of Apollo, which are much too rough and spiky on the soles of my feet. Please see to it they are replaced with smoother cobbles as soon as possible so my friends and I can walk the streets in comfort.

Woof woof,
Reborn Citizen of Athens
Pithos 4b
Temple of Apollo Road
Athens

## THE FACTS

While no other letters have survived, Diogenes was likely the subject of countless complaints in Ancient Athens. He famously lived in poverty, rejected material possessions, and liked nothing more than to make well-to-do citizens feel uncomfortable.

Not much is known of his early life, other than that he was born in around 404 BCE in Sinope (now in Turkey), where he got into some trouble counterfeiting or defacing coins with his father, who was a banker. Whatever happened, the pair were exiled for their crimes and Diogenes wound up in Athens, the epicenter of Greek culture and politics, where great thinkers such as Socrates, Aristotle and Plato debated over questions of virtue, knowledge, truth, and who said which clever quote first. Diogenes, stripped of possessions and citizenship, was particularly drawn to the teachings of Antisthenes, a former pupil of Socrates, whose harsh criticism of pleasure, possessions and social conventions would've made even a lowly maggot feel guilty for their privilege.

Unlike many of his contemporaries, Diogenes felt that giving talks and handing out pamphlets was simply not enough. As well as living in a pithos (a large stone jar) and refusing to get dressed, he performed philosophical stunts, famously wandering around the city holding a lamp up to people's faces in broad daylight, telling them he was looking for (and not finding) "an honest man." Sadly, this was at a time when walking briskly past and pretending to be on an important phone call was not a reasonable excuse.

In addition to harassing passersby, he poured scorn on many of his fellow philosophers, pointing out the contradiction of Plato's teaching and extravagant lifestyle. While Diogenes left little or no writing—pens were an egregious luxury—his peculiar antics were referred to by many other writers (although these letters provide an invaluable addition to this body of evidence).

It's a wonder anyone liked the guy, but over time, the local nuisance attracted a dedicated following, a sandal-less gang who called themselves the "Dogs" or *kynikoi*. It is from them we get the word "cynic," and the Ancient Greek school of philosophy known as Cynicism. While it is impossible to say exactly how many birthday parties and extravagant soirees they ruined, experts predict they could number in the hundreds.

It's not known exactly what Diogenes got up to in later life. He may have been captured by pirates and sold as a slave in Corinth, where, according to the prolific historian and biographer Plutarch, he met the great military leader Alexander the Great. Apparently Alexander was excited to meet the infamous philosopher, and asked him if there was anything he could do for him, as a gesture of his admiration. Diogenes said there was: "Move out of the way, you're blocking the sun."

Unfortunately for those who found him intolerable, Diogenes made it to the ripe old age of 81, or thereabouts, dying in around 323 BCE. Some say he became ill from eating a raw octopus or an ox's foot or from an infected dog bite, while another account has it he simply held his breath until he expired. Whatever led to his demise, he is said to have instructed that his corpse be thrown over the city walls and fed to the stray canines beyond. Even in death, the Dog Philosopher would live up to his name.

## 2.

# *The Vestal Virgin*

Some 300 years after Diogenes shook the pillar of the Parthenon, Rome was embroiled in a scandal. Before the age of emperors, the Eternal City was a sophisticated and complex republic, governed by superstitious men who needed someone to blame when things went wrong.

The best scapegoats, already tried and tested for many centuries, were the Vestal Virgins, a group of priestesses responsible for maintaining the sacred fire that burned at the center of the forum in the Temple of Vesta. The flame symbolized the safety and sanctity of all of Rome, and it was thought if it went out, or if one of its dedicated attendants broke their vow of chastity, *bad* things would happen.

In 75 BCE, bad things happened, and so logic followed that one of the Vestals must have been up to no good. In time-honored tradition, 20-year-old Priestess Licinia was brought before judges in the Roman basilica, and put on trial.*

---

*The trial was held at the pontifical college in Rome and was presided over by the Pontifex Maximus (chief high priest) Plotius. "Trial" seems to have meant something different in Ancient Rome. By this stage, the objective of the court was mainly to further incriminate the Vestal, her conviction being the much-desired outcome.

No details of this salacious ancient courtroom drama were thought to have survived, up until September 2023, when an official transcript was discovered in a marble boxfile beneath the ruins of the Roman Forum. For the first time ever, historians were able to study a firsthand account of the scandalous affair, and discover just what had sent the people of Ancient Rome into a frenzy all those years ago.

---

*Principal persons in the case of PRIESTESS LICINIA vs ROME:*

PRESIDING JUDGE: *Pontifex Maximus*
ACCUSED: *Priestess Licinia, Vestal Virgin*
DEFENSE: *Lawyer representing the Accused*
PROSECUTION: *Lawyer representing Rome*
CLERK: *Assistant to the Presiding Judge*
JURY: *Members of the Roman council*
GALLERY: *Civilian spectators*

LOCATION:
*The Roman basilica, an impressive vaulted room in white marble and pink granite complete with public gallery, Judge's podium, witness dock, stepped seating for the jury and opposite stations for the prosecution and defense.*

## TRANSCRIPT (translated from Latin)

*(Public gallery at full capacity in anticipation of today's sentence. Jury all present beneath the Presiding Judge's seat. Prosecution laughing and joking with friends on the floor. Defense frantically searching through piles of papyrus. Accused cutting a brooding figure with arms crossed, wearing a traditional white gown and showing some leg)*

CLERK: All rise.

*(Everyone stands. Presiding Judge enters courtroom, supported by Clerk. Presiding Judge sits)*

CLERK: Please be seated.

*(Everyone sits. Clerk takes Presiding Judge's walking stick)*

PRESIDING JUDGE: Now, where were we?

*(Clerk whispers to Presiding Judge)*

PRESIDING JUDGE: Ah yes, the Prosecution is to question the Accused. Please begin.

*(The Accused stands up from the Defense table and is escorted to the dock. The Defense gives two thumbs up and mouths, "Good luck." Prosecution brushes crumbs off his belly, stands, straightens out his toga, ambles to center and clears his throat)*

PROSECUTION: Licinia. May I call you that?

ACCUSED: Yes, that is my name.*

PROSECUTION: You are a Vestal Virgin, yes? A priestess of the goddess Vesta?

ACCUSED: That is correct.

PROSECUTION: And it is your job, with five other Vestal Virgins, to guard the sacred flame of Vesta and ensure it does not go out?

ACCUSED: Among countless other duties, yes.

PROSECUTION: Licinia, can you tell the court what happens if a Vestal Virgin lets the flame go out?

ACCUSED: It is thought that if the flame goes out, Romans will be in danger.

PROSECUTION: And you agree that that would be a bad thing, yes?

ACCUSED: It depends which Romans.

*(Member of the gallery snorts. Glares all round)*

---

*The trials of the Vestal Virgins were one of the rare examples in legal history where women were allowed a voice, being permitted to provide testimony in court. However, even then their words were normally read by a male orator defending them.

PROSECUTION: Licinia, I would like you to cast your mind back to last Wednesday. According to this rota . . .

*(Prosecution holds up a stone slab)*

. . . you were on duty all afternoon. Is that correct?

ACCUSED: That is correct.

PROSECUTION: From 2 pm to sundown, it was your sole responsibility to watch the flame. However, at 3 pm, you went out.

*(Gasps and muttering in the gallery)*

What were you going out for, Licinia?

ACCUSED: I had to buy some flowers for the afternoon ritual. Our supplier was sick so I had to fetch them myself.

PROSECUTION: And in going to fetch these all-important flowers, you abandoned your post and left the sacred flame in the care of a trainee Vestal. A young girl not yet qualified to be on active duty.

*(Tutting and head-shaking)*

ACCUSED: I figured she had the sufficient qualifications to stand still and watch a flame for five minutes.

PROSECUTION: Can you tell the court, in detail, what happened when you *finally* returned?

ACCUSED: When I got back to the temple* to continue my shift, Trainee Vestal Fabia informed me the flame was looking a little weak. I fed it some kindling and it soon returned to full health. Everything was fine.

PROSECUTION: Antonius Cleanus, temple janitor, has a different version of events. He says Trainee Vestal Fabia accidentally set fire to her robe while trying to warm her hands at the hearth. As she flapped wildly at her sleeve, she accidentally extinguished the sacred flame, thus endangering all of Rome. On realizing her catastrophic error, she began running in circles around the room shouting, "Kill me, kill me now."

*(Loud gasps and muttering, someone says, "Think of the children!")*

ACCUSED: I'm afraid Mr. Cleanus is mistaken. The flame was weak but not extinguished upon my return to the temple.

PROSECUTION: May I suggest your loyalty to your fellow Vestals is distorting your memory of events?

ACCUSED: You may suggest that, yes. But you would be mistaken.

---

*The Temple of Vesta was a circular building located in the Forum of Rome, originally built by legendary king Numa Pompilius. At the heart of the temple was the central hearth of Vesta which held the fire that burned continuously, supposedly to protect the people of Rome. As this predates modern fire safety regulations, it should come as no surprise that the temple burned down and was rebuilt several times over the course of its history. The remains standing today were reconstructed in the 1930s.

PROSECUTION: Could it also be that, in light of your delicate condition, you have misremembered events?

ACCUSED: I'm sorry, what condition are you referring to?

PROSECUTION: The condition of your being a woman.

*(Male grunts in assent)*

ACCUSED: . . .

*(The Accused squeezes the bridge of her nose. The Prosecution licks his finger and flicks through a stack of papyrus)*

PROSECUTION: Being a Vestal Virgin is an enormous privilege, don't you think? Most women would do anything to be in your sandals.

ACCUSED: Yes, I am very grateful. Thank you.

PROSECUTION: When you were eight years old, a group of illustrious men made a decision that would change the course of your entire life.

ACCUSED: I was very fortunate to have no say in it.

PROSECUTION: After a decade in training, as is the custom, you recently began your decade of active service. You are famous here in Rome. Revered and respected, at just 18 years old. You sit in the best seats at the arena, right beside the Senators. You are at the front and center of countless festivals and events. I even invite you to my famous bacchanalia party every year but you never show up, despite it being a very exclusive event that most people would *die* to attend.

*(The Prosecution takes a moment to compose himself)*

You enjoy privileges no other women can enjoy. You are able to buy, sell, rent and inherit property. You, free from your family, can liberate slaves, own land and even testify in court, where most women must stay silent. You have the honor of serving the Goddess Vesta for 30 glorious years. And what price must you pay in return?

*(Silence)*

ACCUSED: . . . Sorry, was that a rhetorical question?

PROSECUTION: I am asking you.

ACCUSED: I must not love another. I must remain pure and unsullied and not covet so much as a kiss.

PROSECUTION: Indeed.

*(The Prosecution reorganizes his documents. The Accused takes a sip of water. Murmurs flutter through the gallery)*

COURT ADJOURNS FOR ELEVENSES

*(Prosecution tries to remove cherry stains from his toga and stands)*

PROSECUTION: Licinia, does the name Marcus Crassus mean anything to you?

ACCUSED: Unfortunately, yes, it does.

PROSECUTION: The statesman and general purported to be the richest man in Rome?*

ACCUSED: So he keeps telling me.

PROSECUTION: Can I inquire as to the nature of your relationship with General Crassus?

ACCUSED: Yes. We don't have a relationship.

PROSECUTION: But you have been spotted together on numerous occasions?

ACCUSED: He has a habit of hounding me.

PROSECUTION: Just last week you were seen together, what is it—

*(Prosecution consults notes)*

*General Marcus Licinius Crassus (115–53 BCE) was known as the richest man in Rome. He had made a fortune in property, supposedly by buying houses on the cheap, then rebuilding them with slave labor. He went on to carve out a major military and political career, brutally quashing the slave revolt of Spartacus and forming the First Triumvirate (political alliance) with Pompey the Great and Julius Caesar. A Trump-like figure of the Roman world, he developed a reputation for ruthlessness and greed. He also might've been Licinia's first cousin.

—seven times. On the most recent occasion you were witnessed entering a building together. Coincidentally, on the very same day, there was a verruca outbreak in the local baths.

ACCUSED: On the day in question, General Crassus came to my home to apologize for his previous doggedness. As Vestals, we are taught to act with grace and humility, so, believing him to be genuine, I invited him inside for refreshments. However, once inside, the general's ulterior motive became clear.´

PROSECUTION: An ulterior motive you were all too happy to pop off your stola and facilitate!

*(Gasps. An old man faints. Defense stands)*

DEFENSE: Objection!

PRESIDING JUDGE: Overruled.

*(Defense sits down)*

ACCUSED: Sir, if I had a type, which I don't because it is forbidden, it would certainly not be angry-looking men with beady eyes and thin lips. No offense to you, of course.

*(Prosecution touches his thin lips)*

ACCUSED: And regardless, the general did not want to have sex with me, thank goodness.

*(Another old man faints)*

He was asking me, for the 800th time, to sell him my countryside villa.

*(Disagreeing murmurs)*

He's been pestering me for months, trying to get it at a discounted rate. The man won't take no for an answer.

PROSECUTION: Just to be clear, you are telling the court the richest man in Rome has been courting, if you don't mind me saying, the most . . . attractive . . . of the Vestals—

*(Accused rolls her eyes)*

—not for sexual gratification but in order to secure the purchase of a countryside villa?

ACCUSED: That is what I have been telling you all, ad nauseam, for days.

*(Stifled laughter in the gallery)*

PROSECUTION: Priestess, why would a man who already owns half of Rome exhaust himself in such a pursuit?

ACCUSED: Because he wants to own all of it. The man has been snapping up property from desperate landowners for years.

*(Nodding and muttering in the gallery)*

PROSECUTION: There are plenty of desperate landowners to take advantage of. Why pursue a financially solvent Priestess of Vesta?

ACCUSED: Because he *really* wants my villa.

PROSECUTION: And what makes your villa so irresistible?

ACCUSED: To Marcus Crassus? It's got a swimming pool in the shape of Venus's breasts.

*(Gasps. The first old man faints again)*

PROSECUTION: Right. And can you describe, in detail, these *breasts?*

ACCUSED: Breasts are these soft body parts beneath a woman's clothing . . .

PROSECUTION: Yes, yes, I know what . . .

*(The Prosecution frowns and grumbles unintelligibly)*

. . . So you're telling the court Marcus Crassus, the eminent dignitary and celebrated general, wants your villa because it's got a pool in the shape of some breasts?

ACCUSED: Also because it sits in-between two plots he already owns, so he's probably looking to turn it all into some kind of awful resort or something.

PROSECUTION: And is that why you declined?

ACCUSED: I declined because his offers were laughably low. And then I declined again and again, and continued to decline every time he cornered me. Ask him, he'll tell you.

PROSECUTION: Well, that might be difficult, Priestess, since General Crassus has no intention of cooperating with these proceedings. I think his exact words were, "How dare you bring this farce to my doorstep? I shall not legitimize your ludicrous case with my presence."

ACCUSED: If only I had a penis and could say the same.

*(Suppressed laughter)*

COURT ADJOURNS FOR LUNCH

*(Prosecution stands. Half a sandwich falls from a fold in his toga)*

PROSECUTION: Priestess, can you recall the date of your first encounter with General Crassus?

ACCUSED: I suppose it must have been about six or seven months ago.

PROSECUTION: Was it perhaps on 18 September of last year, when local cake vendor Bacillus Bakerus witnessed you together in the Forum?

ACCUSED: It was probably around that time, yes.

PROSECUTION: Indulge me for a moment, and let us presume you're a classy girl and waited until your second or third date, at the end of the month, before you locked lips with the general.

*(Gasps)*

DEFENSE: Objection!

PRESIDING JUDGE: Overruled.

PROSECUTION: This would correlate rather curiously with the shocking disappearance of 27 sheep from a local farm, their skeletons later found stripped to the bone.

ACCUSED: Yes, that was me.

*(Detecting heavy sarcasm from the Accused)*

PROSECUTION: I'll give you the benefit of the doubt and posit that full-blown intercourse didn't occur until 7 October.

*(Bigger gasps)*

ACCUSED: What happened on 7 October?

PROSECUTION: This is a very serious matter, Priestess.

ACCUSED: No, please, I am genuinely intrigued.

PROSECUTION: Well, it just so happens that on that day, my cousin was feeling a bit poorly.

*("Awwws" from the gallery)*

ACCUSED: I see. Well, I suppose it all adds up then.

PROSECUTION: Indeed. And you continued your sexual adventures, wreaking havoc on the innocent civilians of Rome, until last Wednesday, when the Goddess Vesta, after enduring months and months of insult and impiety, finally reached the end of her tether and, through Trainee Priestess Fabia, extinguished the sacred flame for once and for all.

*(Lamenting sighs. One woman mutters, "It doesn't bear thinking about!")*

This timeline of impropriety correlates, with frightening precision, to countless other unfortunate events that have affected innocent Romans and, indeed, Rome as a whole. Events that, I propose, were a direct result of your unchastity.

ACCUSED: I suppose you will read a list now.

PROSECUTION: I shall. In chronological order, omitting those already mentioned, I hereby accuse you of causing the loss of a battle in the Sertorian War* in December last year, for causing the loss of a skirmish in the same war in January . . .

*The Sertorian Wars were a series of civil wars fought between 83 BCE and 72 BCE and named after the statesman and military commander Quintus Sertorius. At the time of the trial, Rome was facing considerable challenges to its authority and squabbles among political factions, which would ultimately lead to the fall of the Roman Republic. Had Licinia kept the sacred flame of Vesta burning, however, all of this could have been avoided.

*(Gasps mounting with each incident)*

. . . for Marcus Tullius Cicero's two-week headache in February, Lucius Licinius Lucullus's veranda renovation woes in March, Gaius Julius Caesar's kidnapping by pirates in April, the loss of a further two Sertorian War skirmishes between May and June, me stubbing my toe so hard it made me cry in July and lastly for making it rain the day my wife got her hair done in August.

ACCUSED: I regret everything but the toe.

PROSECUTION: And who's to say what hardships await us in the coming weeks, now the temporary extinguishing of the flame has snuffed out whatever was left of our good fortune?

*("It doesn't bear thinking about!" again)*

ACCUSED: I'm sure some bad things will happen, yes, but I can't in good conscience take all the credit. Sometimes, obviously very rarely, bad things happen because of *men*.

*(Scoffs and boos)*

I take my role as a Vestal Virgin very seriously. While I had no say in my initiation, I dutifully accepted my calling. I have had no adolescence. You relinquished it for me. Yes, I am spared your unhappy marriages and the thankless servitude you demand. But I am also exempt from love, forbidden a first kiss, excluded from what I gather is one of the greatest pleasures in life. This is not a sacrifice I take lightly. I have made it every day for ten years, and shall make it every day for another 20, should truth prevail. I serve the Goddess Vesta. I tend to the sacred flame of Rome. And it will take more than a rich, thin-lipped bore to shake my devotion.

*(Impressed muttering. One person starts clapping but is quickly silenced)*

PROSECUTION: A rousing proclamation, Priestess. However, gentlemen of the court, I am left unconvinced. It is my sincere belief that the Priestess has broken her vow of chastity and is spinning a web of lies to deceive us. She provides no actual evidence to verify her claim that her encounters with General Marcus Crassus were strictly business-related. The only person who could substantiate her version of events has refused to cooperate, on the grounds of this trial being a "farce."

*(The Defense drops his head in his hands, sighs loudly and mumbles, "Well, that's it then" to himself)*

Her story does not hold up to scrutiny. It is a desperate cover for a long list of wrongdoings. Wrongdoings that dwindled and eventually extinguished the sacred flame of Vesta, and threatened the sanctity and safety of Rome.

*(The Defense, sighing repeatedly, has started packing his briefcase)*

Therefore, I encourage the traditional sentence, consistent with the severity of the crime. Priestess Licinia should be buried alive in a sealed underground chamber with the customary pitcher of water and snacks.* There, as she spends her final days in darkness and solitude, she may sit and think about what she has done. And as she draws her last breaths, perhaps the gods will find it in their hearts to forgive her.

*(Commotion at the back of the courtroom. A man with slicked-back hair and a pin-striped toga has entered and is conferring with officials. A chain of whispers finds its way to the Presiding Judge who listens stoically)*

PRESIDING JUDGE: A surprise witness wishes to take the stand!

PROSECUTION: Objection!

PRESIDING JUDGE: Overruled!

*(Excited gasps and murmurs. The Prosecution sits down, flapping angrily. The Accused returns to sit next to the Defense. The Surprise Witness takes the stand)*

PRESIDING JUDGE: Would the Defense like to cross-examine the witness?

DEFENSE: Umm, no thank you, we're all right, I think.

---

*Vestal Virgins accused of impurity were once stoned to death but from the sixth century BCE onward, the punishment was changed to a live burial as no one wanted to be responsible for spilling the blood of a sacred woman. After a funeral procession, the accused would be placed in an underground vault with, as Plutarch wrote, bread, water and oil, along with a bed, blankets and a lighted lamp.

*(The Accused says something angry and unintelligible to her Defense and stands up)*

ACCUSED: *I* would like to cross-examine the witness.

PRESIDING JUDGE: I advise you to take counsel from your representative, Priestess . . .

ACCUSED: He's fired. I am representing myself.

*(The Defense scoffs. The Presiding Judge's eyebrows reach for his hairline)*

PRESIDING JUDGE: Very well.

*(The Defense crosses his arms and sulks. The Accused takes the floor and addresses the witness)*

ACCUSED: Would you please introduce yourself to the court, Mister . . . ?

SURPRISE WITNESS: Estatus, Cassius Estatus—Rome's foremost estate agent currently offering o percent commission on all property purchases in the—

ACCUSED: Thank you. And you work with General Marcus Crassus, I presume?

SURPRISE WITNESS: Yes, I manage his property portfolio and facilitate new purchases.

PROSECUTION: Objection! What has General Crassus's property portfolio got to do with anything?

PRESIDING JUDGE: Overruled!

ACCUSED: Has General Marcus Crassus mentioned a desire to expand his property portfolio recently?

SURPRISE WITNESS: He is always looking to expand his property portfolio.

ACCUSED: The plan is to own all of Rome, is it not?

SURPRISE WITNESS: Yes, but we're not supposed to tell anyone.

ACCUSED: Does this plan for city-wide domination include the suburbs?

SURPRISE WITNESS: Yes it does.

ACCUSED: Does it include my villa in the suburbs?

SURPRISE WITNESS: I'm afraid so, yes.

ACCUSED: And has General Marcus Crassus asked you to facilitate the purchase of my villa in the suburbs?

SURPRISE WITNESS: Many times, yes.

ACCUSED: How many times?

SURPRISE WITNESS: 138 times.

PROSECUTION: Objection! Where is the evidence?

PRESIDING JUDGE: Sustained. You must present evidence to support your claim.

ACCUSED: Mr. Estatus, did the general make any of these requests in writing?

SURPRISE WITNESS: Yes, he sent 98 letters. I have them right here.

*(The Surprise Witness brings out a stack of papyrus)*

PROSECUTION: Objection!

PRESIDING JUDGE: Overruled!

*(The Prosecution's face now resembles a ripe tomato)*

ACCUSED: Mr. Estatus, would you care to read your letters to the court?

SURPRISE WITNESS: Of course. *(Reading)* Cassius, are you getting these? I really want that horrible little Vestal's villa. The one with the pool in the shape of Venus's boobs. Make it happen. Marcus.

*(Gasps and whispers)*

(*Reading another*) Cassius, HELLO! Why haven't you got that ratty Vestal's villa yet? The one with the boob pool. I want it as a cheeky hideaway for my mistresses. Don't tell the wife! Haha. Anyway, make it happen ASAP. Marcus.

(*Another*) Cassius, just saw that prudish little brat again. She won't budge! I want that villa! The one with the boob—

ACCUSED: Thank you, that will be all.

(*The Accused walks confidently back to her seat. The Prosecution buries his head in his hands. The gallery erupts in excited chatter*)

PRESIDING JUDGE: Order! Order! I've heard all I need to hear.

(*The Presiding Judge organizes his notes*)

PRESIDING JUDGE: Gentlemen of the court. You have brought Priestess Licinia before me under the suspicion of a terrible crime. A crime that carries with it the maximum sentence: live burial, without parole.

(*Grave mutters and mumbles*)

However, I find accusations of the Accused's unchastity unfounded. Have we not all been on the receiving end of General Crassus's incessant badgering at one point or another?

(*Many of the older gentlemen nod*)

It seems to me this young lady is just another one of his victims.

*(The Presiding Judge puts away his notes, looks out at the courtroom. Spectators in the gallery hold their breath)*

Therefore, in the case of Priestess Licinia, Vestal Virgin and guardian of the sacred flame vs Rome, I find the defendant not guilty of unchastity and hereby close the case against her.

*(The courtroom erupts in cheers. The Accused leans back smiling. The Prosecution kicks the table, stubbing his toe so badly it makes him cry)*

## THE FACTS

Whether it's Pandora in Greek mythology, or Eve in the Judeo-Christian tradition, women have long been blamed for ruining everything. In Ancient Rome, the enviable position of the people's scapegoat was formalized in the eighth century BCE, with the inauguration of the first priestesses of Vesta. The institution survived for over one thousand years, before being shut down by Christians in 391 CE, who found other people to blame.

But before the Romans sent their pagan gods packing, the Temple of Vesta was about as important as it got. Hungry for prestige, noble families jostled to have their prepubescent daughters chosen to be one of the exalted six to guard the sacred flame, so it's likely Licinia's mother was an insufferable bighead the day her daughter was accepted into the College of Vestals in 85 BCE at the precocious age of between six and ten. Over the next decade, Licinia would have learned her many duties, before serving as a fully fledged priestess alongside her five colleagues, until her retirement twenty years later.

As high-profile figures in Rome, Vestal Virgins were frequently referenced by ancient writers, particularly when they met with scandal or appeared in court. The case of Licinia and her apparent intimacy with Marcus Licinius Crassus received particular attention. Plutarch, who clearly had a very low opinion of Crassus, summarized the case: "Licinia was the owner of a pleasant villa in suburbs which Crassus wished to get at a low price, and it was for this reason that he was forever hovering about the woman and paying his court to her . . . " The ruthless reputation of Crassus ultimately led to her acquittal as the Presiding Judge, the Pontifex Maximus, could well believe Crassus was motivated by greed not lust.

While trials against Vestals were relatively rare throughout the college's existence, many of those hauled up before the Pontifex Maximus were not as lucky as Licinia. Some were used as convenient scapegoats for military disasters or crises, as happened to the Vestals Opimia and Floronia, who were found guilty of unchastity in 216 BCE after Hannibal and the Carthaginians annihilated the Romans. In 472 BCE after a pestilence caused many pregnant women to miscarry, the Vestal Orbinia was convicted of immorality and sentenced to death. Unsuitable, immodest behavior could also lead to accusations, as was the case with Postumia in the fifth century BCE when she was tried for wearing overly extravagant clothes and, according to Plutarch, was "too bold with her jokes in front of men."

Like Licinia, Postumia was acquitted, although she no doubt learned to keep her jokes to herself. As for Crassus, he rose to become an enormously powerful general and statesman—funding Julius Caesar's early career and forming an alliance with him—before meeting his end in a battle against the Parthians in 53 BCE. Stories later emerged that the victorious Parthians poured molten gold into his mouth in mockery of his greed, and then decapitated him and used his head as a prop during a performance of Euripides' Greek tragedy *The Bacchae*.

Before his death, Licinia did eventually cave and sell her countryside villa to the greedy general. Presumably, after years of relentless nagging, she'd finally had enough. It is not known whether Cassius Estatus facilitated the sale, or came through with his 0 percent commission offer, nor is it known what Licinia did after the unfortunate episode.

At the end of their 30 years of service, retired Vestals were free to love, have sex and get married, although few of them did. After what they put her through, it seems likely that, by the time Licinia was eligible to be with a man, she was put off them altogether.

## 3.

# The Plague

In the 14th century, Europe woke up to the first glimmers of the Renaissance. About 800 years prior, the mighty Roman Empire, picked apart by invasions, corruption, debts and Jesus, finally said "sod it" and packed it all in, plunging the entire continent into what's commonly been known as the "Dark Ages" (someone wasn't watching the flame).

While most historians now disagree with this term (because apparently lots of things did happen in the Dark Ages), it was still a bit of a rubbish time to be alive, especially if you were born at the tail end. Europeans kicking about in this unfortunate period had to endure one of the worst pandemics the world has ever known: the Black Death.

For centuries, "the Plague," the disease behind it all, remained frustratingly private. But in 2022, a once-in-a-lifetime opportunity presented itself to London journalist Denis Pepys—an exclusive sit-down interview with the harbinger of misery herself.

---

I arrive early at a private members' club in central London where waiters are serving much-needed coffee to hungover creatives, early bird entrepreneurs and other assorted insufferables. It's Sunday morning and regrets from the night before seem to swirl about the head of a famous actor hiding in the corner. He gobbles down a minimalist full English breakfast in the hopes of quietening his spiraling, Margarita-muddled mind. He catches me staring and shoots me a look, at which point I realize it's just an ordinary man and my speculations are totally unreasonable.

But in this exclusive haunt, being famous isn't unusual. Many stars come here to get away from the riffraff outside (and to be seen getting away from them), which I suspect is why my subject, the Plague, chose it. While she is no longer splashed across the tabloids and hot on the lips of the masses like some of her modern imitators, she is an indelible part of our history and was a household name for many centuries.

She floats in on a green-golden glow (15 minutes late) and takes a seat in the armchair opposite. A waiter arrives almost immediately with an extra-hot, triple-shot Americano and a glass of sparkling mineral water.

"Lovely to see you again, Ms. Pestis," he says, putting down the drinks and hurrying away.

I look at her quizzically and she knows what I'm thinking: "It's my scientific name. *Yersinia pestis*," she says. Nearby, a nose-ringed man in a fisherman's beanie looks up from his MacBook Pro, head tilting, eyes squinting. He goes back to his computer and searches "Cool scientific version of Duncan."

Yersinia has only been interviewed once before. My great-great-great-great-great-great-great-great-great-great-great-grandfather Samuel Pepys* did a whole feature on her for the

---

*The London diarist Samuel Pepys was famed for writing about the plague outbreak of 1665 and the Great Fire of London the following year, once

*London Gazette*, but on print day the Great Fire of London tore through the city and the piece went up in flames.

Now, through some bizarre, protracted nepotism, I am here to pick up his mantle. I confess I am feeling rather intimidated to follow in the footsteps of one of history's greatest chroniclers, but Yersinia puts me at ease.

"I'm sure you'll do just fine, darling," she says. "Just don't make the same mistake and ask me my age."

I ask why she agreed to be interviewed now, after so much time out of the limelight.

"Don't make me change my mind," she says, unsmiling.

I bow my head, like one might bow to a queen. And who can blame me? Yersinia is microbe royalty. Perhaps the most famous disease there ever was.

I reach for my notepad and try my hardest to stop my hands from shaking.

"Yersinia, you've been about a long time," I say. Her eyebrows rise as she takes a sip of coffee. "And you've touched millions upon millions of lives. Would you mind starting from the beginning, and telling me how it all began?"

She sighs, and I immediately know she's been asked the question a thousand times. I apologize just as many times, and fumble with my notes as though I have a better opener prepared.

Yersinia elegantly lights a cigarette, prompting a trainee

---

he'd finished burying his cheese. He seemed to have a morbid fascination with the disease, visiting the plague pits in Moorfields and keeping a close eye on weekly mortality bills. He remained in the city throughout the outbreak and to keep healthy he chewed tobacco and avoided wearing new periwigs, both futile measures, although he never contracted the disease.

waiter to march over. He is quickly intercepted by the manager who whispers something in his ear and sends him on his way. Yersinia takes a long drag.

"You want to know about my time as *Yersinia pseudotuberculosis?*"* she says.

"If that's all right," I stutter.

"It was dull, dull, dull. But we all have to start somewhere."

"And is that why you chose to evolve?"

Yersinia's transformation from *pseudotuberculosis* to *pestis* remains a blueprint for mild but ambitious pathogens everywhere, and she is forever inundated with invitations and requests to impart her wisdom. She tells me just yesterday she received a handwritten letter from a fledgling young bacterium desperate for advice on how to make it big.

"If you have to ask," she says, "then it's not going to happen."

But it wasn't all rainbows and pustules overnight. Even as the more virulent *pestis*, Yersinia still had to pay her dues.

"I cut my teeth in Asia. In small mammals, rats mostly. Hardly glamorous, but it got me ready for my big break."

Her big break, of course, was her ingenious move into humans. A move that would change the course of her life, and our lives, forever.

"How did you come up with it?" I ask.

"I didn't," she says. "It was Natasha." She looks out of the window and I see a bittersweet montage of memories flicker past her eyes. "She pitched me world domination and I said, 'Sign me up, doll.'"

---

*Yersinia pseudotuberculosis* was a relatively mild gut pathogen, from which the much nastier plague-carrying *Y. pestis* evolved within the last few thousand years.

Natasha, I learn, was Yersinia's first agent. An entrepreneur, philanthropist, patron of the arts and flea. Natasha believed in Yersinia when no one else would.

"That darned flea was the best there was. And she wasn't afraid to get her hands dirty."

In fact, it was Natasha who made that historic leap, transporting Yersinia from a rat into her first human being.

"She took a big bite out of an old man's buttocks and that was it. I was in."

As infected rats died, their hungry fleas followed Natasha's example and made the switch to human blood. And just like that, Yersinia's career snowballed.

"It wasn't long before I'd worked my way around the whole village. And since you humans just love to travel, I was in Constantinople before I knew it. And, well, you know the rest."

"Yes, the Justinian plague, 541 CE.* Your first big hit. How did that make you feel?"

"You know, for so long we—and by 'we' I mean every other organism on Earth—had to sit back and watch while you guys had all the fun. It was like there was this great party going on and none of us were invited. And suddenly, because of Natasha, I was the belle of the ball."

Her eyes light up and I know she is being transported right back.

"How would you describe those early days?" I ask.

"Golden. They were golden." She is almost lost in the reverie, but sees me and remembers to elaborate. "I saw everyone,

---

*The Justinian plague, named for the Byzantine emperor Justinian I, tore through Constantinople (now Istanbul) from 541 CE and spread throughout western Europe.

I did everything. I was in the tavernas and the workshops, the brothels and the palaces. I was at the parties and the dances and the weddings. Oh, it was everything they say it was and more."

She leans back, bathing in a nostalgic glow.

"And what was the reaction from your peers? I imagine some of them were quite jealous of your new life?" I say.

"Oh, no doubt. They all came out of the woodwork. Some pathogens I hadn't spoken to in years were suddenly sending flowers and asking me out to brunch. Others . . . well, they just got bitter."

I ready my pen to take down a name. She notices.

"It's no scoop, sweetheart. It was just *Dirofilaria immitis,* an old girlfriend. Or Dog Heartworm as she goes by now. She sent me a vicious letter accusing me of forgetting where I'd come from."

"Had you forgotten?"

"Have you ever been in a rat's anus, honey? You'd want to forget too."

We both have a little laugh, and I wonder if she is warming to me. Did she have a laugh with Grandpa Pepys?

Perceiving the seed of a friendship, I consider abandoning my next line of questioning, but then remember that she is the actual plague and I am a serious journalist.

"So you were enjoying being a part of our world. Was the feeling mutual?" I ask.

"Whatever do you mean?" she says, squinting.

"Well, the people of Constantinople welcomed you into their lives by showing you fun, affection, family, community. In return you gave them fever, headaches, swollen lymph nodes, muscle pain, tissue necrosis and, more often than not, death," I say, avoiding eye contact.

The warmth evaporates and I immediately wish I'd just asked her about her plans for the weekend.

"The coffee here is . . . isn't the coffee here great?" I say, sipping my rancid oat flat white.

"Look, I regret the death part," she says, finally. "Killing your host is never ideal. But you do what you need to do in order to survive."

"Not just survive, flourish!" I say. "You were flourishing."

"Well, if you say so," she says with her best bashful smile.

"Of course, the Justinian plague was just the beginning. A spectacular debut, but not your magnum opus. That came nearly a thousand years later with the 'Black Death.'"

She nods politely and checks her nails. I wonder if I have made a faux pas, but carry on regardless.

"I suspect no microbe will ever surpass what you did in Europe in the 14th century. It was a pandemic like no other. You saw off at least 25 million people."

"Fifty million," she interrupts.

"Sorry, 50 million. By any measure, between half and two thirds of the population."

While I am talking, Yersinia summons one of the waiters and orders another extra-hot, triple-shot Americano. I indicate that I am still working on my oat flat white and try to remember what I was saying.

"Of course, if you order an Americano in Italy they'll laugh you out of town," she says before I can continue. "Social suicide. Have you ever been?"

"Yes, Rome and Florence," I answer.

"Isn't Florence a dream?"

"You know it well?" I say, fully aware she'd spent enough time there to wipe out half of its residents.

"It was best mid-Renaissance. I did a string of small, independent outbreaks. Arthouse stuff. Some of my finest work."

"But surely nothing compared to the outbreak of 1348, at the height of the Black Death?" I ask.

"I remember this one tour I did of Rome, in 1522. Michelangelo was there. Grumpy little man but his work was just sublime. I left him to it, of course. Though I don't think he ever quite surpassed the *David*. God, Natasha would've loved the *David*. Have you seen it?"

I shake my head.

"You mean to say you went to Florence and didn't see the *David*? Well, darling, you must go back immediately."

I reach for the reins.

"Venice, Genoa, Barcelona, Paris and London were also huge plague hotspots, not to mention many smaller cities, towns and villages across Europe. You brought an entire continent to its knees in record time. Was there a plan, or were you just making it up as you went along?"

Yersinia's Americano arrives but it is not hot enough. The drink is quickly recalled and brought back steaming, by which time neither of us can remember the question.

"Sorry, darling, what did you want to know?"

I check my notes.

"I was wondering whether the Black Death was all planned out beforehand, or if you were sort of improvising as you went along?"

"Planned, I guess, I don't know. Can we talk about something else?" she says, sighing.

I fumble and can almost hear Grandpa tutting from the heavens.

"It's just all so dreadfully boring," she complains as I try to think of something to say.

"But it's your crowning achievement. Your greatest work!"

"Dull, dull, dull," she says, looking out of the window for something more interesting. I thumb through my notepad, quickly skipping past 16 other newly embargoed questions.

Fortunately, Yersinia's publicist, also a flea, followed up later with the following email:

Apologies, I believe there might have been some crossed wires. Yersinia prefers not to discuss BD—she finds it all so dreadfully boring. Please refer to the below press release for the information you require. [. . .]

By summer 1348, Yersinia had taken Europe by storm, garnering critical acclaim. The *Florence Tribune* described her performance as "devastating" and the *Paris Herald* lauded her as "the second most painful way to die" (after being flayed alive by a butter knife).

Released in several powerful variants: bubonic, septicemic and pneumonic, Yersinia could be transmitted through a cough, a sneeze or a drop of blood. This three-pronged approach made the Black Death one of the fastest-growing and most fatal pandemics in human history.

It starts raining outside and we spend a few minutes discussing the discrepancies between reality and the morning forecast. I can tell she finds this conversation just as dull, but it's buying me some time to figure out what to say next.

As she graciously answers a question about average rainfall where she lives, I wonder why the architect of such a famous and successful pandemic is so reluctant to discuss it. I do understand her boredom. She must have spoken about it endlessly for centuries, and aren't all stars sick to the back teeth of talking about their greatest hits?

But I can't help but think there is another reason.

Channelling some long-forgotten confidence, I abandon a tedious story about rising damp and jump back in.

"You like humans, don't you?" I say.

She squints. "Excuse me?"

"You said your time in Constantinople—at the weddings and dances, among the people—you said they were the golden days. What did you mean by that?"

"Well, it was all so new and exciting."

"You were young and naïve, I suppose. Not yet aware of what you were capable of. Of the kind of devastation you could inflict."

"Is that a question or a statement?" she purrs.

"Tell me if I'm out of line here," I say, voice trembling, "but I wonder if the reason you don't like talking about the Black Death is because it hurts to remember being so despised by the very humans you wanted to be around. It hurts to know that by joining the party, you shut it down."

She stares at me for what feels like a lifetime, and then, just before I panic and backtrack on everything I've said, calmly lights another cigarette.

"You're forgetting that I'm a malevolent pathogen."

"I don't believe you," I say, smiling.

She scoffs and returns to the safety of the window. Her eyes film over. The smoke curls toward the ceiling.

"There was a boy," she says finally. "Pierre."

I wait for her to continue.

"It was 1399. Things were slowing down." She takes a big drag. "We met in a tiny village in the south of France. The second I laid eyes on him I said, 'Boy, I could give it all up for you.' And so I did. I moved in, fell head over heels, and within a week, he was dead."

We sit in silence.

"Yersinia, I—"

"Have you tried the Bloody Marys here?" she says, clicking her fingers. I lean in, desperate not to lose her.

"Pierre, was he—"

"No more of that! We're having cocktails," she interrupts. I explain that I never drink on the job, but she calls me dull, and I have to accept.

"Two Marys, you know how I like it," she says to a waiter, who scurries away like a terrified woodland creature.

"Did you ever meet her? Bloody Mary?" I ask.

"Queen Mary I? I was all over her. But she was asymptomatic. Not so much as a sneeze."

I see a spark come back and don't want to lose it.

"You must've had quite a few famous victims over the years," I say.

"Well, I don't like to name-drop but . . . " she says, leaning back into it. "Do you know Alfonso XI, the King of Castile? He was in the middle of the Siege of Gibraltar,* terrible timing.

*King Alfonso XI of Castile had the misfortune in 1350 to be the only European monarch to succumb to the plague. At the time he was attempting to retake the fortified town of Gibraltar from Muslim rule, and refused to end the siege despite a breakout of the plague in the Castilian camp. Everyone around him begged him to call off the attack but he was adamant they carry on until Gibraltar was Christian again. He died of the disease on 26 March and Gibraltar remained in Muslim control.

But then I always did like throwing a spanner in the works," she smiles. "Nice place, Gibraltar."

"Do you have a favorite, out of all the places you've visited?"

"Oh no, I couldn't possibly choose," she says.

"Or is there anywhere you wished you'd gone, that you weren't quite able to get to?" I ask.

"Well, Antarctica would've been fun, but no human habitation means . . . no way."*

She laughs, but I sense a glimmer of regret, sorrow for a life not lived. I realize her predicament. She is wholly reliant on the lives and movements of others. Always the guest, never the host.

The Bloody Marys arrive just in time. We both take a sip and I notice it's almost entirely vodka with the tiniest splash of tomato. I go dizzy and my confidence soars.

"After the Black Death you continued traveling Europe, although we were beginning to get you under control. You popped up in China in the mid-19th century and from there spread worldwide. Your swansong, I suppose. But then, a steady decline. The conditions in which you thrived—the squashed, insanitary settlements where humans and animals lived cheek by jowl—got cleaned up. We learned about hygiene, about contamination and infection. And nowadays your outbreaks are very rare indeed. There are occasionally a few isolated incidents, the odd mini flare-up in small communities,

---

*The third plague pandemic, which emerged first in Yunnan, China in 1855, spread to Hong Kong by 1894 and across the world, including the Americas. In India and China alone, it killed around 12 million people. Until global warming opens up a lucrative real estate opportunity, Antarctica remains the only continent unaffected.

but with modern medicine, you are treatable. You are no longer a threat."

Yersinia blinks at me over her Bloody Mary, and for a moment I think she might get up and leave. Something stirs in her, an ambiguous sadness finally recognized.

"Well, you do know how to make a girl feel special, don't ya?" she says, voice cracking.

We're interrupted by a fan who comes over, shivering like a baby deer.

"I'm so sorry, I never normally do this," says the middle-aged woman. "But I'm a doctor and I just had to say, I think the way you colonized and reproduced in the lymph nodes was simply amazing. It's like—wow! You were incredible."

Yersinia thanks her and signs an autograph (she doesn't do selfies).

"Are you still working? I feel like I haven't heard about you in a while," says the fan.

As Yersinia gracefully navigates the unintended slight, I can't help but feel sorry for her. It's a bitter pill to swallow, knowing your best days are behind you. She once ruled the world, striking fear into the hearts of all mankind. Now she lives only in the history books, her centuries-long reign of terror reduced to a chapter, the morbid fascination of a few.

But while Yersinia's star fades, her kin are very much on the rise. Every year a bright-eyed young microbe launches their career, hoping to make it big.

I look across at the hand sanitizer dispenser fixed to the wall, Duncan engaged in a video conference call next to us and the terrified-looking lady wearing a face mask in the corner, and wonder what Yersinia thinks of a certain pathogen following in her footsteps.

"Oh yes, she was good," she says, eyeing up a QR code stuck to the table.

Yersinia lights yet another cigarette, the wistful turn in our conversation taking its toll. I let the silence run its course.

"Do you miss us?" I ask, finally.

She pauses and watches her cigarette smoke spin ribbons in the air.

"I miss the resolve. Some of you can smile in the face of anything."

I know she is talking about Pierre, but I don't dare ask. I check my watch and realize we are coming to the end of our allotted hour.

"Just some quick-fire questions, before we finish . . . if you don't mind?" I say. She nods.

ME: What advice would you give to your younger self?

YERSINIA: Never stop believing, because one day, darling, you are going to rule the world.

ME: What's the last song you listened to?

YERSINIA: "Simply the Best" by Tina Turner. I listen to it every morning.

ME: If you could collaborate with anyone in your field, who would it be?

YERSINIA: Salmonella. I love what's she's doing in chicken.

ME: Who would you want to play you in a movie of your life?

YERSINIA: Dame Judi Dench.

ME: Any regrets?

YERSINIA: I wish I had taken Natasha out for one last dinner, to say thank you for everything.

ME: Favorite film?

YERSINIA: *Cars 2*.

ME: Favorite way to travel?

YERSINIA: There's nothing like riding a big old sneeze all the way into someone's mouth.

ME: Favorite memory?

YERSINIA: Lying in a wheat field with Pierre, counting the stars, just before he erupted in boils and pustules.

ME: Which historical figure would you have most liked to infect but didn't?

YERSINIA: Margaret Thatcher.

ME: How do you like to wind down at the end of a long day?

YERSINIA: I like to sit on the veranda at my home in Provence, sipping a Martini, listening to the birds.

ME: Plans for the rest of the day?

YERSINIA: I'm meeting Tonsillitis for lunch, and then we're going shopping in Harrods.

And with that, Yersinia gets up to leave.

"So who did it better, me or Grandpa?" I ask, half-jokingly.

She puts on a pair of huge Dior sunglasses.

"Well, put it this way, sweetheart, Grandpa didn't take the cocktail," she says.

I insist on paying the bill, but she tells me they never charge her here. We shake hands and she disappears into Soho, green glow trailing behind her.

Over the next couple of days a strange feeling comes over me—a comedown, perhaps—from my encounter with one of the most notorious historical figures of all time. As I scramble to finish this feature before my deadline, an unrelenting headache thumps at my forehead and a fever pumps through my veins. Eventually the boiling blood spills out into tender lumps and bumps on my skin.

In search of some antibiotics, I limp past the private members' club to find it boarded up. A gaggle of disgruntled creatives check their phones for somewhere else to go in front of a giant red "X" painted on the door.

I chuckle, and in the process cough out several vital organs. "She's still got it," I say, picking up my liver.

## THE FACTS

*Yersinia pestis* is a legend among pathogens. In her heyday she could tear through populations and kill millions, with only the variola virus—smallpox—ever matching her in virulence.

Her most common mode of transmission was, and still is, to hop a ride on a rodent, infecting it and any fleas it might be carrying. A flea bite could then transmit the bacterium to a human, leading to bubonic plague and an all-too-certain death if left untreated. Outbreaks of plague have occurred since at least 3000 BCE but the first recorded epidemic broke out during the reign of the Byzantine emperor Justinian in around 541 CE. Originating in China, Yersinia probably spread to Africa and then to Constantinople (now Istanbul) via ships carrying large amounts of grain and rats from Egypt. Once in Constantinople, the disease killed as many as 10,000 people a day before spreading throughout western Europe over the next two centuries.

The plague would erupt again in the 1300s, sweeping through China and Asia from around 1334, before reaching Europe, probably via Sicilian ports, in the late 1340s, when it became known as the Black Death. In an era before hand sanitizer and face masks, the preferred method of hygiene was to sniff vinegar and encourage children to smoke. Unsurprisingly, this public health campaign had limited success, and it would take at least a couple of centuries before population levels recovered.

Not quite ready to retire, Yersinia flared up again in Asia in the late 19th and early 20th centuries. It was during this outbreak in 1894 that the French-Swiss bacteriologist Alexandre Yersin, while examining the fluid from plague-ridden buboes, discovered which bacterium was responsible, and Yersinia—which he described as "small stocky spindles with rounded ends"—was finally identified.* The discovery turbocharged advances in treatment and diagnosis, and the subsequent introduction of sulphonamides and antibiotics greatly reduced the severity and frequency of plague outbreaks.

Yersinia may have left the world stage, but she does still pursue arthouse projects, with occasional cases reported in Africa, Asia, South America, the US, and even—if some accounts are to be believed—in small pockets of central London.

---

*Yersinia, once she was identified, went through several name changes. Until 1900 she was known as *Bacterium pestis*, then *Bacillus pestis* until 1923, when she became known as *Pasteurella pestis*. It wasn't until around 1970 that she was designated the name *Yersinia pestis*. It is of course the time-honored tradition of global icons to change their names. Such rebranding is a bold move, with varying results; although in Yersinia's case, it's clearly been a success.

# 4.

## *The Master's Ferret*

Once the plague had finished decimating Europe, new life rose from the ashes. In Italy, the rebirth (or Renaissance) saw a partial return to the glory days of Ancient Greece and Rome, where art, science and technology were seen as good things, rather than the evil instruments of the dark lord Satan.

In 1490, 38-year-old Leonardo from a town called Vinci was working as court painter, sculptor, architect, engineer and all-round handyman for Ludovico Sforza, the Duke of Bari, soon to be Duke of Milan. Although yet to create the masterpieces for which he is known today (namely a certain Ms. Lisa), Leonardo was already considered a master, revered and respected throughout Italy and beyond.

For centuries, historians have tried to demystify the enigmatic genius through the paintings, sketches and notebooks he left behind, and in 1978, Baltimore's foremost psychic medium took it one step further.

In front of local journalists and regional news crews, Juliet P. Matthews attempted to make history by summoning the spirit of the Renaissance master, but accidentally got connected to a 500-year-old ferret instead. Thrilled to have been contacted, the ferret immediately started telling its life story, and the medium, too embarrassed to admit her mistake, stayed on the line to listen.

Below is that story, translated from Italian-ferret, with nonsensical squeaks redacted.

---

It was on the job, flushing a family of rabbits out of their twisting burrow in the woods, when I first realized I was unbelievably good looking.

The mother rabbit had frozen in front of me, and inside her wide, petrified eyes, I could see an iridescent hunk so gorgeous I quite forgot what I was supposed to be doing. He was long and slender with toned arms, a chiseled face and a coat so white it was almost blinding. Standing there in stunned silence, strangely turned on, I soon realized the vision was in fact me, reflected in the rabbit's tears.

"I must be immortalized," I whispered to myself as I preened in her terrified, twitching eyes.

With no time to waste (ferrets rarely live past six), I parted ways with my handler and traveled to Milan with nothing but my outrageous good looks and a dream, and, because I was so breathtakingly beautiful, it wasn't long before I was scouted by a modeling agent. Signor Serragli was the best in the business and had a whole host of animals on his books. He repped the horse from Ambrogio de Predis's *Adoration of the Magi,* the dog from Dario di Giovanni's *Abduction of Helen from Cythera* and even did some pro bono work for the Lion you might remember from Zanetto Bugatto's *Saint Jerome and the Lion**

---

*All real Renaissance paintings by prominent artists based in Milan or northern Italy. By the end of the 15th century, Milan had become one of the

(this was a sore point as Serragli and the lion fell out over some hairy commission negotiations and never spoke again).

Signor Serragli had grown weary of the same old projects and was excited to sink his teeth into my career. In my first year I modeled for Butinone, Foppa and Solari. The best in the business. With each job I would spend a month or two with the artist, building a rapport, posing for studies and maquettes and then when they were done with me, I'd be sent back off to Signor Serragli. Sometimes I was glad to go back, other times it was heart-wrenching. When you work on a painting with a whole studio of artists and assistants, you become a family.

As the seasons changed, so did my look. In winter my coat was a magnificent, brilliant white and in summer, a handsome gray. To my initial surprise, I was booked twice as often in the summer months, but it didn't take me long to figure out why.

In the industry we have something called a "focal point," an area of interest or emphasis that attracts the viewer's eye first and foremost. For whatever reason, most artists like this to be a human, usually the baby Jesus with a receding hairline. Any element of the painting that distracts the viewer from the focal point (like yours truly in white) is invariably removed during the final stages. It seems in winter I was simply too gorgeous, too mesmerizing, too magnetic to remain in the frame, and so

---

most important economic and political centers of Europe. The immense riches of the city are reflected in the huge number of iconic artworks that were commissioned by its wealthiest citizens. Giovanni Ambrogio de Predis (c. 1455 to c. 1508) collaborated with Leonardo da Vinci on the *Virgin of the Rocks* altarpiece in Milan, and he and the artist Zanetto Bugatto (1440–76) worked for the Sforza dukes of Milan. Dario di Giovanni (1420–95), based in Padua, was known for his religious work.

ended up getting scrubbed out of almost all the pieces I worked on.

Regardless, after a few years of grinding and networking I had built solid relationships with all but one of the major studios in Milan. My no less beautiful summer coat won me spots in more and more finished pieces, and gradually I grew content with being blended into rural landscapes and pastoral vistas. I was pleased to be working, pleased to be wanted, and in the excitement of the castings and sittings, exhibitions and parties, I almost forgot why I had come to Milan in the first place. All the while, time continued its march, and before I knew it, I was five.

"I give him another year, if that," I overheard Signor Serragli say to his assistant one evening in July. The next day he signed two replacements.

The threat of my mortality lingered in the stifling heat of summer. Signor Serragli said it was likely my last.

In the night, I would seek solace in the cool air by the window and watch the stars twinkle in the blue. The injustice stung. They were half as beautiful as me, I thought, and yet they got to shine on forever. I watched for the shooting ones and wished upon all of them.

"Studio of Leonardo," said Signor Serragli, reading an inquiry letter to his assistant one balmy morning in August. "Wants a ferret. Principal role."

"Foreground?" I said, jumping to the front of my cage.

"Foreground, apparently," said Signor Serragli.

The other ferrets came forward to audition, rattling the bars as they struck their poses.

Signor Serragli sat and watched us, arms crossed, grunting in approval when we impressed him and wincing when we didn't. I gave it everything. Head poised, eyes squinting and lips pursed, I demonstrated the length of my body, the rippling muscles in my arms and the fluid curve of my supple spine. The younger ferrets never stood a chance.

Through the winding Milanese streets we went, under the gaze of frozen gargoyles sitting on intricate stone arches above. The towering spire of the cathedral, reaching above the yellow haze, dipped out of view as we passed the sun-drenched stained-glass windows and squinted through their multicolored glow.

We twisted down another narrow alley and left along a row of fine houses, their wealthy owners stepping out resplendent in velvet robes and fur-trimmed gowns, and then through the markets with their sweets and spices. I covered my nose as we approached the barrels of pepper and cinnamon, as I always did, but the smell was too strong and I sneezed anyway.

Finally we reached the Sforzesco Castle and, passing the guards, moved across the Corte Vecchia, where the clacks and clangs of hammers and chisels echoed through the courtyard, the Duke's in-house artisans hard at work. Through the corridors and past the humming workshops we went, holding our breaths through lingering clouds of marble dust, until we came to a door marked with an "L."

Signor Serragli swung and released the brass knocker, sending a loud snap up the spiraling staircase within.

"Ferret, for Messer Leonardo," said Signor Serragli, handing me over to the angelic-looking boy who opened the door.

"Okay," said the boy, snatching the cage and holding it carelessly in his arms. He stared at me with his big green eyes while I adjusted myself in my newly tilted world.

"Payment on deliv—" began Signor Serragli before the door was slammed in his face.

I strained to steady myself as the boy leaped up the stairs. By the time we reached the top of the dark stairwell, I was uncharacteristically disheveled and a little dizzy. I stroked down the stray fur behind my ears, dropped my chin and sucked in my cheeks, ready to meet the master.

The boy shouldered through another door and into great beams of light. A wave of fumes rushed up my nostrils and pickled my brain, the intoxicating tang of turpentine making everything spin.

I had never seen a room so alive. All about the tables and workbenches, boys busied themselves with their tasks.* Two youngsters stretched canvas over a wooden frame, another one pored over thick volumes in the corner, studying sketches and diagrams. Along a paint-splattered workbench, three older boys diligently mixed colors and, behind them, running between the stools and easels, younger ones laughed and wrestled, evading a telling-off from the supervisor who chased after them.

Up the walls, creaking shelves reached all the way to the high ceiling, overflowing with weird and wonderful curiosities: anatomical models, skulls, artifacts, something called a "helicopter" and a small wooden sign reading "Live, Laugh,

---

*It's a sad truth that some of humanity's greatest achievements were only made possible by the abundance of child labor. In Renaissance Milan, it was common for young boys to take work as a *fattorino*, helping out with menial labor for the brilliant artists who were flourishing in the great city. While Leonardo's name was immortalized in history, most of the impoverished children who helped him were soon forgotten.

Love." Piles of paper spilled over the sides, their edges fluttering in the breeze that came warm and gentle through open windows.

Everywhere I looked there was color. Potted plants with their magnificent flowers, hanging fabrics and abandoned masterpieces peeking out from neat stacks waiting to be finished. All of it bathed in gold, all of it shimmering.

The boy dropped the cage on a table and reached in to grab me, squeezing my ribs much too tight. I squealed.

"Careful, Salaì!" came a warm voice. "We must be gentle." Long, slender hands rescued me from Salaì's grasp and wrapped themselves lightly around my chest. I saw at once the inquisitive, sparkling eyes, the long nose and neat, glossy beard. He had a handsome face, framed with wavy locks, curling down to strong shoulders draped in fine robes. For a moment I wondered if the turpentine had sent me loopy and that I was, perhaps, just looking at a painting.

"Is that a rat, Messer Leonardo?" asked a beautiful young woman sitting on a stool by the window. I gasped and went to correct her. But Messer Leonardo stroked my head and suddenly I wasn't bothered.

"A ferret, Signora Cecilia," he said.

He lifted me into a sunbeam and gently stretched me out, inspecting the length of my body and the shine of my coat. I can't remember ever being held with such care, such reverence. It felt wonderful.

"Where do you want me, Messer Leonardo?" I said, trying to remain professional when all I wanted to do was fall asleep in his hands.

He carried me over to Signora Cecilia.

"You want me to hold it?" she said, wincing.

"He is well-tempered. A true professional," said Leonardo, passing me to her.

She took me cautiously, her hands cold and uncertain.

"I'm happy to pose without a holder, Messer Leonardo," I said, a little annoyed Signor Serragli hadn't informed the studio that one wasn't necessary. Holders were for wrigglers.

"He is not a wriggler," said Leonardo, lifting my two arms onto Cecilia's upper arm and placing her hand lightly on my back. I decided not to question his methods. He was the master, after all.

Once she realized I wasn't going to bite or scratch, Cecilia finally relaxed. Perhaps, in her time as a holder, she'd come across my badly behaved peers and received a nip or two. Not all ferret models were as professional as me. She was right to be cautious.

I lifted my face to the light and smized.

"Wonderful!" said Leonardo as he stepped back behind his canvas and began to draw.

Cecilia and Leonardo must have worked together before, for they got on well and nattered all the way through the sitting. I chimed in occasionally, laughing at their jokes and grunting in approval whenever appropriate, but otherwise kept quiet. One must remain professional, especially in the early stages.

"Salaì?" said Leonardo, catching the boy before he ran off to make trouble.*

---

*Gian Giacomo Caprotti da Oreno (1480–1524) entered Leonardo's studio at the age of ten as an apprentice to the great painter. Despite his angelic looks, his mischievous side quickly became apparent and he was given the nickname "Salaì," or "little devil" in Tuscan slang. Despite his naughtiness and minimal art skills, Leonardo was enchanted by Salaì's cherubic looks and kept him employed for more than 25 years, and even left him half his vineyard in his will. The well-behaved studio boys must've been furious.

"Yes?" said Salaì.

"Some Vin Santo for our guest."

"No, thank you," I said. "I never drink on the job."

Salaì came back with a glass of wine for Cecilia, spilling a little as he hastily set it down beside her.

"And the cantucci," said Leonardo. Salaì dragged his feet away and returned, half-stomping, with some small biscuits for Cecilia to dip into the wine. I politely declined, of course. It's all very well for the crew to indulge, but the model must always watch their figure.

Salaì ran away before he could be called on again, his long blond curls dancing behind him.

"Well, at least he's beautiful," said Cecilia. Leonardo smiled. "You must pay them well."

"Just bed, board and sustenance, like all the studios," said Leonardo, studying the line of my shoulder.

"And sweets?" asked Cecilia. Leonardo looked up at her, squinting. "His tongue is bright red, Messer Leonardo."

Leonardo turned to look for Salaì and his felonious red tongue, but the little devil was long gone.

"At least that solves the mystery of the missing florins," said Cecilia, smirking. Leonardo sighed and shook his head.

"He's a rogue and rascal. But I can't bring myself to be rid of him."*

---

*Leonardo's letters and diaries are packed with complaints about the young Salaì's behavior. The boy stole repeatedly, using the money for sweets, and caused endless damage inside the studio. A brutal description of the young pupil can be found scrawled in the margins of one of Leonardo's letters: *"ladro, bugiardo, ostinato, ghiotto"*—"thief, liar, obstinate, glutton"—but he never did get rid of him.

"I expect the duke is having the same dilemma," said Cecilia, beginning to stroke my back.

"I don't think so, Signora," said Leonardo. "Your very presence here proves he is besotted."

"For now," she said.

Cecilia, it turns out, was the Duke of Bari's favorite mistress. Why she was working as a holder is anyone's guess. Perhaps the duke didn't give her much of an allowance.

"Shall we call it a day?" said Cecilia, shaking out her fingers. The sun had traversed the sky and turned the whole room orange, but Leonardo was caught in a trance, utterly obsessed with me. I was no stranger to attention, but this was different. It was as though everything else had been plucked from existence, and all that remained was me, him and his canvas, suspended in the nothingness. I remember wishing it were true.

"Messer Leonardo?" said Cecilia. Leonardo looked up at her as if he had just been snatched from a dream.

"Oh yes, sorry, yes, of course."

Salaì was called.

"Find him somewhere to sleep," said Leonardo, passing me to him. "And be gentle, remember?"

Salaì carried me roughly across the room, looking for a box, but after no more than a few moments searching, gave up and dropped me on the floor. He ran off to continue testing everyone's patience, leaving me to figure out my accommodation for myself. In any other studio, on any other job, I would've kicked up a fuss. But my afternoon with Leonardo had been the stuff of dreams, and not even the questionable hospitality could bring me down. I found a pleasant spot high up on the shelves in between a sheep's skull and an old foot bath, and,

letting the delicious fumes make my head tingle, curled up for
my beauty sleep.

The week rolled on with its long, uninterrupted mornings and
golden afternoons. We worked every day, not resting until the
sun touched the horizon, or until Cecilia wanted to go home.
I had never seen a holder work such long hours.

"Same time Monday?" asked Cecilia, getting up at the end
of the week.

"I was going to suggest a break, actually," said Leonardo,
putting down his brushes.

"Oh. Okay," said Cecilia, disappointed. She must have enjoyed our company.

"Sometimes the best way to work on a painting is to not
work on it at all," said Leonardo.

"May I see it?" asked Cecilia. I knew never to ask to see an
artist's work before it was finished. They hate that. Leonardo
was no different and reeled off all sorts of disclaimers.

"Of course, it's all going to change," he said, leaving space
for Cecilia on the other side of the easel. She got up and went
to stand beside him, taking me with her.

"Oh . . . " I said, trying my best to hide my surprise. There
I was in the foreground, as expected, but, controversially, Leonardo had decided to keep Cecilia in the frame and, by the
looks of things, had spent much more time working on her
than me.

"You've painted the holder?" I said. "That's . . . interesting."
I hadn't wanted to come across sarcastic and quickly corrected
myself. "Innovative, is what I mean."

"It is much more interesting with the ferret, Messer Leonardo, you were right," said Cecilia. She gestured to the lower half of the canvas. "This part looked so empty before." Before? I had no idea what she was talking about.

It had been a long week, so it didn't strike me as odd for Leonardo to take a break from the painting. Artists need time to recharge if they are to successively capture beauty on canvas, and it wasn't unheard of for them to spend a few days on a side project so they could come back to the main event with fresh eyes. Any good model, however mesmerizing, knows they must fall into each studio's particular rhythm.

Unfortunately, Leonardo's rhythm was difficult to decipher, no matter how hard I studied it. Over the following days, I watched as he flitted between countless other projects, never being able to stick with just one. He'd start work on something, a sketch for a painting or a diagram of a body, and then spot a bird gliding above the rooftops outside. He'd become obsessed, consult his skeletons, sketch their wings, make calculations and then just as easily become enchanted by the colors of a leaf or the way the light was falling through a window. From my vantage point over the whole studio, I could see as clear as day the trail of unfinished projects he left in his wake.*

I endeavored to get his attention, confident the sight of me would reinvigorate his passion for the portrait. I draped my-

---

*Leonardo's brilliance was matched only by his skills of procrastination. He often imagined and started projects only to abandon them halfway, leaving a trail of incomplete paintings, sculptures and works. His notebooks, amounting to tens of thousands of pages, were filled with sketches, designs and thoughts on a huge range of topics from engineering and warfare to perspective, geography and philosophy. He was fascinated by everything, and so no single thing could keep his attention for long. Some historians speculate he had ADHD, although we'll never know for sure.

self elegantly against a canvas, leaned mysteriously on a stack of books and twirled seductively around a pot of brushes. I was spellbinding, hypnotizing, irresistible, but impossibly, none of it worked. I wondered if he might've gone blind. I had seen it happen before.

After four days on hiatus, the painting was beginning to gather dust, and I started to think I was involved in some sort of elaborate practical joke. There was no other explanation for it, until Leonardo stood before the easel one evening and sighed.

"Salaì?" he said, noticing the boy loiter. He invited him forward and ruffled his hair. "Be honest. What do you think?"

Salaì put his hands on his hips and tilted his head.

"It's ugly," he said. I gasped.

"All of it?" asked Leonardo.

"No. Just him," said Salaì, pointing at me sitting in her arms.

It all stopped, the whole world screeching to a halt.

"Ugly," he said. Ugly! No one had ever called me ugly. How could I be ugly? Surely someone would have told me! Perhaps I'd misheard, I thought. He couldn't possibly have called *me* "ugly"!

"It's the fumes," I reassured myself. "The fumes have sent me mad." I took some deep breaths and tried to compose myself, but the spiral took me anyway, and that night, as rain battered the windows and drowned everyone's snores, I climbed down the shelves to see for myself.

The moonlight, faint and blue through the heavy clouds, fell upon the canvas. I stood before it and tried to see what Salaì saw. Slowly, like a nightmare, it emerged from the oils: the thin, spindly body, the pointy snout and the beady eyes. I saw it now, the dull gray fur, the ratty paws and the misshapen, wonky ears.

If you'd told me then that my heart had been ripped from my chest, or that I was dead or inside out or that I had never been alive at all, I would have believed you.

Ugly. I was ugly.

How had I been so deluded? How had I ever thought I was beautiful? How foolish to think I could make it in the foreground!

"DELETE IT!" I screamed into the darkness, the monstrosity looming over me. "I'M UGLY!"

I climbed, dazed and bereft, back up high, somewhere no one would have to endure the sight of the most hideous creature in the world, but only made it to the third shelf. There, beside the skeleton of a bird and a wooden sign reading "Beauty is on the inside," I fell asleep, half-hoping I would never wake up again.

It was the soft scratch of chalk that alerted me to the fact that, despite my sincere wishes, I was still alive. My eyelids were a brilliant red and I was warm, wonderfully warm. Lifting my head, I squinted through the light and found the master there, right in front of me. His face sharpened with every blink, his kind, inquisitive eyes and gentle smile emerging from the blur.

"But master, we must work on the new commission," said one of the older studio boys as Leonardo ran his chalk across the paper, capturing the new curve of my raised head and the shadow it cast across my body.

"Just a few more," he said, turning the page in his sketchbook. The studio boy went off grumbling. I lifted my face to the light, as I had always known to do.

"Yes!" said Leonardo, capturing it all, obsessed. His sudden, burning interest stirred something inside of me. I sucked in my cheeks and smized.

"YES!" said Leonardo.

For the next half an hour we went back to that place, the nothingness where only he and I existed. "Yes! YES!" he cried as I gave him my famous pouting corkscrew.

The blissful 30 minutes passed, and he was close to figuring out how to best revisit the abandoned portrait, studying the way my paws looked when bent this way or that, when a buzzard swooped past outside and stole his attention.

He put down his chalk and sketchbook and started for the window, busy mind filling with thoughts of flight. In an instant I saw my bones scattered in the dirt, each rib gnawed away by the rain and the insects, all sinking into obscurity with each passing year until no one would be certain I was ever alive at all. He must continue, I thought, or I shall be lost.

Possessed and desperate, I leaped forward and bit him hard on the pinkie finger. He threw me off, sending me flying. "I deserved that," I thought as I smashed into a pile of books.

"Oww!" he cried, sucking his finger. I crawled back onto the shelf and resumed my pose, half-expecting to spend the rest of my life in a cage, defanged and muzzled. But he just stared at me, astonished, and I could tell by his eyes he understood. He picked up his sketchbook and chalk and got lost in me again.

From then on, I was invited to live on Leonardo's desk (the studio boys converted an open crate into a mini apartment) and I would sit and watch the master as he worked. It didn't bother me for him to engage in other pursuits in between our sessions, just so long as he finished them. If a new fantasy caught his fancy at an inopportune time, I would gently nibble his pinkie finger and remind him of the task at hand. In those few days he completed a fine series of sketches of me, a design for a new flying machine and a 1000-piece jigsaw puzzle. He was buoyed by an unfamiliar sense of accomplishment and was spurred on to work even harder.

Autumn came, and then the first whispers of winter. It was a crisp morning in November when I was awoken by a gasp. I opened my eyes and sat up in my shoebox bed. The master stared down at me, eyes wide. I looked at my coat to see sprinkles of white. We stared at each other and smiled.

A message was sent to Cecilia, asking her to come in for a sitting as soon as possible. The imminent arrival of my winter coat sent Leonardo into a frenzy. He was excited about the portrait again and couldn't wait to get to work.

I turned it up a notch at the gym, using some toothpicks with stones glued to the ends, and by the time Cecilia arrived a fortnight later, my coat was white as snow and I had the body of Adonis (the ferret version). I don't think I ever looked so good in all my life.

"So you've figured out how to make it work?" asked Cecilia, setting herself down on the stool and straightening out her dress.

"I have indeed!" said Leonardo, adjusting his easel.

"A new ferret?" said Cecilia as Salaì came over and placed me in her arms.

"Same ferret, new clothes," said Leonardo.

Leonardo dipped behind the canvas and got back to work. In the hours that passed, he barely looked at Cecilia, and the only paint on his brush was white.

Cecilia came in every week after that, pleased with the

steady progress after months of stagnation.* Leonardo's interest didn't dwindle, and every session he would delight in explaining his plan for my nose, for her dress, for the shimmering film of her eye or the bulge of my biceps. His thoughts would spill excitedly from him and they were infectious. I even got comfortable enough to start making suggestions.

"Perhaps a touch of vermilion for her cheek?" I'd say. He wouldn't reply, but when he dabbed his brush in the bright red paint I knew he had understood.

The young Cecilia asked question after question, about Milan, war, flight, anatomy, the ocean, the heavens. As he spoke we sat in silence, eager to learn everything he had to tell us. And when he inevitably found himself getting distracted, all I had to do was open my mouth and mime a soft bite for him to regain his focus. With procrastination at bay, the painting came along in leaps and bounds. And by March, he was finished.

We all stood looking at it. Leonardo, Cecilia and me.

"You have outdone yourself, Messer Leonardo," said Cecilia. Leonardo looked at the floor, forever uncomfortable with compliments. I tried to say something, anything, but the words piled up in my throat.

"It's beautiful," is all I managed.

If I could have the moment again, I would tell him it was

---

*Leonardo finished the *Lady with an Ermine* far more quickly than many of his other paintings. The *Mona Lisa*, for example, took over 15 years to complete. His main commission during his Milan years was to be a colossal bronze equestrian statue in honor of Sforza. By the time he was ready to cast the sculpture, however, war had broken out, and the Italians agreed the metal would be better used to blow up the French.

perfect. I would ask him how it was possible. How it was possible he could have paused it all, all that life and the readiness in my arms and the warmth of her cheeks. How had he known that this went here and that went there, that the light had fallen how it had and the glow had done what it had done to her eyes? How had he seen all this between the noise, in the middle of all that moving and spinning and changing? I would ask him how he had stopped the clocks. How he had persuaded time to halt its march, just for me and her. I would make him tell me.

"Where will it go?" asked Cecilia, sadly. I learned during our final sittings that the Duke of Bari had commissioned the painting but now, for whatever reason, didn't want it.

"You must take it with you, it is yours," said Leonardo. I was flattered, honored, floored. But then I looked at Cecilia and knew I couldn't take it.

"It is Cecilia's," I said. "It has to be." She had been so down since the duke ended their relationship, and her fears of fading with time were just as sincere as mine. Besides, it wouldn't have fitted in my cage at Signor Serragli's office. Better to go to her house and be seen by her friends and visitors, and then perhaps, after some time, find its way to a place where everyone could look at it.

The studio boys carefully packed it into a wooden box and sent it away with Cecilia and a servant. As I watched them from the window, getting into their carriage and disappearing into the chaos of Milan, I realized that I was done. I would never model again. I would never see another season. My bones were aching. I was six.

. . .

The following day, Signor Serragli came to collect me.

"What will you do with him?" asked Leonardo, holding me in his arms.

I knew what was facing me when I returned to Signor Serragli's. I had seen it happen to the other animals in their twilight years.

"I'll sell his fur. If I skin him before he grays I can get a few florins for him," said Signor Serragli. I imagined my skin stretched across the cuffs of a glove or the trim of a cape.

"I'll buy him as he is. No skinning needed," said Leonardo.

I looked up at the kind eyes and felt my old heart thump.

"Huh?" said Signor Serragli.

I sniffed the air to be sure I wasn't high on turpentine, but all I could smell were the spring flowers carried on the breeze. Signor Serragli walked away with a pocketful of money and an empty cage, chuckling as he went. Leonardo stroked the top of my head, making me shiver. I melted into his soft fingers, those masterful hands touched by the divine, and fell fast asleep.

The days were getting longer now, the pale gray skies turning blue. I drank in every moment there in the studio, watching from my tabletop apartment as Leonardo and the boys shook off the winter lethargy and buried themselves in their work. My white coat was fading for the final time, but all about me was alive with the promise of spring.

I could see young Salaì sat in the corner, bright red tongue poking out while he keenly studied the skeleton of a bird, counting its ribs and drawing them in his sketchbook. Across from him, the older boys ground up rocks and insects on the splattered workbench, producing a fine powder they would later turn into paint. Leonardo was at his desk, drawing a naked man in a circle, his four arms and four legs outstretched and touching the sides. He was buried in it, entirely bewitched, like nothing else existed, until one of the boys came in carrying a newly primed canvas. He turned to look and for a moment, it seemed as if he was filling it with his mind, putting down the outlines in charcoal and layering in the paint. I wondered what he was creating in there—another ferret? The Virgin Mary? Baby Jesus with a receding hairline? Or perhaps it was another young lady, strong and gentle, with a touch of vermilion in her cheek. Whatever it was, I knew it would soon be a masterpiece. But not yet. Leonardo put his pinkie finger to his mouth and gave it a soft bite, before returning his attention to his drawing, and the eight-limbed circle man.

Spring made way for summer, whose warm breeze and golden light made the studio shimmer again. The heat soothed my aching bones, but every day I got weaker.

At the window, over the busy stacks of roofs and spires, I could see the woods and fields where I used to work flushing rabbits out of their burrows. In all my six years, I'd never once thought of returning, but now the countryside called to me, and I longed to answer.

Leonardo noticed and held me in his arms.

"Let's get you home," he whispered.

When I opened my eyes again, we were out in the fields. In a beautiful spot, surrounded by trees, he brought me out of the carry cage and placed me on the ground. It had been a long time since I'd felt earth under my feet. Last time I was just a young ferret, destined to be forgotten like all the other ferrets before me. I returned to the soil immortal, committed to canvas for eternity by the great Leonardo da Vinci.

"It was an honor working with you," I said, my muddled mind resorting to formalities. He nodded, and I knew he understood.

With my job done in the foreground, it was time to join the ensemble. Taking one last look at the man who made me live forever, I scuttled wearily into the bushes and was promptly eaten by a badger.

## THE FACTS

Untitled at the time, Leonardo's masterpiece later became known as *Lady with an Ermine*. Historians are now quite confident the Ermine (a sort of wild weasel) was actually a ferret, as verified by our dear departed model. Swap out the species and rearrange the names in order of importance and the title becomes the much more fitting *Ferret with a Lady*.

*Ferret with a Lady* is one of just four surviving portraits of women by the great Renaissance artist and scientist Leonardo da Vinci (which just means Leonardo from Vinci—a small town outside Florence). The original "Renaissance Man," his full list of skills is too long to fit in any standard-sized book, but in any case, it is through his artwork that he is probably best known today. While he was unmistakably a genius, many will be comforted to know he was also a spectacular procrastinator, constantly switching between projects and forever avoiding the task at hand. He was fascinated by nature and spent much of his time obsessed with flight, anatomy, science, philosophy and mathematics. When he was lost in an infatuation, everything else was pushed aside, much to the annoyance of his staff and commissioners.

Painted between 1489 and 1490, *Ferret with a Lady* precedes his better-known portrait, the *Mona Lisa (without a ferret)*—arguably the most famous painting in the world—by about a decade, although many would argue *Ferret with a Lady* is far more beautiful and beguiling.

The woman in the painting is Cecilia Gallerani (1473–1536), a well-educated, former lady-in-waiting and mistress of Leonardo's patron Ludovico Maria Sforza, the future Duke of Milan. It is thought Leonardo wanted to feature an ermine, an animal long considered to represent purity, and likely used a ferret in its place for practical reasons. The domesticated animals were much more professional than their wild cousins, and larger too.

Recent examination of the layers beneath the finished masterpiece have revealed the Italian artist painted the work in three stages. His first version was a simple portrait with no animal; the second attempt included a ferret in its gray summer coat; and the third featured a stunning, muscular, white one.

Historians believe the "ermine" may be a reference to the first portion of Cecilia's surname, *"gale,"* which means weasel or ermine in Greek. Some theorize the animal was a covert representation of the duke, who had been granted the Order of the Ermine, a type of knighthood, the macho-looking beast seemingly protecting Cecilia, who was possibly pregnant at the time (by May 1491 she had given birth to the duke's son).

In the end, all this duke-pleasing was for nothing because, by the time the portrait was finished, he didn't want it. It's not every day one turns down an original Leonardo, but the duke's new wife discovered the relationship and wanted Cecilia gone, and the placating husband probably thought better of keeping her picture knocking about. The duke continued to provide for his ex-mistress, and when she went on to marry another noble, he bought them a palace as a wedding gift.

*Ferret with a Lady* is thought to have remained with Cecilia until her death, at which point no one really knows where it went for a few hundred years. It reappeared in the possession of a Polish prince in the 1800s, and a century later was coveted by the Nazis, who were keen to own the entire Leonardo collection. The Allies hid it during the Second World War, but it was eventually found and confiscated. It bounced around various high-ranking Nazis and ended up hanging in "The Butcher of Poland's" lakeside villa in Bavaria until the end of the war, when it was rescued by the Monuments Men, an elite team set up to recover stolen masterpieces.

After a remarkable and thrilling journey, the portrait finally found its way to the Czartoryski Museum in Kraków, Poland, where it remains to this day. The inordinately good-looking ferret smizes and flexes for thousands of admirers every week, exceeding the average lifespan of its species by more than 500 years.

# 5.

# *The Visitor to Strasbourg*

By the time Leonardo da Vinci blobbed the last bit of paint on the *Mona Lisa,* the Renaissance movement had spread all over Europe. The ordinary people of Strasbourg, however, were yet to enjoy its benefits. Designated a free imperial city of the Germanic Holy Roman Empire in 1262, Strasbourg was largely self-governing, and things weren't being governed well. Starving, diseased and generally fed up, its citizens believed God had left them to rot. The Church, their only pathway to salvation, was corrupt, depraved and full of sin, and everybody knew it. The Pope strutted around his palace dripping in jewels, bishops hoarded money and extorted the poor, priests got drunk and partied, and all of them had sex with whomever they pleased, all the while telling everyone else to be good boys and girls.

Social unrest bubbled against this backdrop of tremendous hypocrisy, but several failed peasant revolts proved resistance was futile. Strasbourg's ruling ministers and clergymen had sold their city down the River Styx, and there was nothing anyone could do about it.

It was in this miasma of doom and misery that a mass hysteria took hold of the condemned souls of

Strasbourg, an absurd affliction that still stumps medical experts to this day.

Until recently, no comprehensive contemporary account of this far-fetched chapter in history was thought to exist, but in 2019, an invaluable document was discovered by workers installing a new solid gold bathroom suite in the Vatican.

Below, originally commissioned by His Holiness Pope Leo X, is a report on the imperial free city of Strasbourg in the year of our Lord 1518.*

---

## CONFIDENTIAL DOSSIER— FOR HOLY EYES ONLY

**By Appointment of His Holiness Pope Leo X**

**Subject:** The imperial free city of Strasbourg, Germany, governed by local magistrates and burghers under the sovereignty of The Holy Roman Emperor

*Monday 22 July, 1518*

After nearly two months of traveling, I arrived in Strasbourg to gather information on the prevailing religious tensions within the city, aiming to understand the depth and nature of the spiritual discord that has taken root among its inhabitants.

---

*Incredibly, while the events described in these pages sound too bizarre to be true, nearly all that follows actually aligns with facts laid out in numerous verified historical records.

First impressions were not so good. As I rolled up through the poorer districts and observed the pale, emaciated residents traipsing around in the gloom, I wondered what wicked things they had done to deserve such terrible punishment. The hallmarks of plague, famine and bad luck presented themselves at every turn, and quite put me off my travel snacks.

On arrival at the town hall, I was welcomed by Ammeister Andreas Drachenfels, first minister of the city, who I found to be charming and courteous in his manner, if not a little distracted. We exchanged the customary gifts. I gave him a couple of indulgence vouchers with which he could expunge two sins of his choice at any cathedral in the Holy Roman Empire. In return, he presented me with a special silver token with which I could redeem one hour with the finest prostitute in the city. I accepted it graciously, but obviously had no use for it, being a pious man who has sworn a lifetime vow of chastity.*

The Ammeister had my bags taken to the guest apartments and let me know I was welcome at all council gatherings, private meetings and events, as is customary for a papal envoy with an all-access pass. I thanked him for his hospitality and went to freshen up and take a nap, arranging to meet him later on.

At lunchtime we reunited and wasted no time getting into the nitty-gritty. We covered a wide range of topics including

*The selling of indulgences supposedly absolved someone of past sins or ensured a clear pathway to heaven after death. Conveniently, indulgences also generated quite a bit of cash for the Vatican. By 1517, one angry German by the name of Martin Luther had decided the whole thing had a whiff of corruption about it and pinned his letter of complaint to the doors of All Saints' Church in Wittenberg. The 95 theses, as they were soon known, would mark the beginnings of the Protestant Reformation.

education, sanitation, trade and social mobility, and their possible relationships with the growing religious disquiet. When we came to the subject of the evident famine, the Ammeister feigned ignorance. I informed him that I had seen the barren fields and hideous, skeletal peasants on the way in, at which point he claimed it to be "news untrue." Harvests had been disappointing, he admitted, but he had high hopes the next one was going to be "so, so good. The best, probably."

It was then that a senior aide came into the room and whispered something into his ear. The Ammeister's easygoing demeanor soon evaporated, and our private meeting was swiftly brought to a close. As he made moves to dispatch me, I politely brandished my Vatican card and reminded him of my ecclesiastical mandate.

I followed the Ammeister through the winding corridors of the town hall, all the way to the stuffy corner office of the Minister for Health.

### *Minutes from the unscheduled meeting between Ammeister Andreas and the Minister for Health*

*(The Ammeister throws open the door, without knocking. The elderly, rotund minister jumps up from the floor, where he has been lying on his back, staring at the ceiling)*

AMMEISTER: TALK!

*(The minister clambers onto his chair, visibly embarrassed)*

MINISTER FOR HEALTH: Ammeister, I—

AMMEISTER: Eight of them now?

MINISTER FOR HEALTH: Fifteen, by the last count.

AMMEISTER: F—k!

MINISTER FOR HEALTH: It would seem so, yes.

AMMEISTER: And what are you doing about it?

MINISTER FOR HEALTH: Well, I—I–the thing is, there's a lot of—thing is I—

*(The Ammeister groans and exits, slamming the door as he goes)*

★

I tailed the Ammeister as he marched off, barking orders at several terrified aides and servants. A special council was to be convened within the hour, I gathered. Still tired from my arduous journey, I agreed to retire to the waiting room while he went on a mad rampage through the building, flinging open doors and screaming at various unsuspecting colleagues.

My curiosity getting the better of me, I started up a conversation with the common servant who delivered me some pastries. Holding a handkerchief to my nose to mask the peasanty smell, I asked if she knew anything about what was going on, to which she replied, "Aye, methinks I've grasped the marrow of it." I showed her my Vatican card and asked her to provide a witness statement.

*Witness statement*
*from the smelly pastry girl*

Well, nigh on a week past, this poor woman, Frau Troffea I thinks, from the meager parts of town, stepped outside her house, quiet-like, and took to dancing. Now, 'tis odd to jig in the street, not least for dance be deemed the devil's own sport, but should it be naught but a hop and a leap, nary a soul will raise a clamor. But Frau Troffea did carry on, hour upon hour, not minding her vexed husband's shouts nor the puzzled looks from a gathering of neighbors.

All of the day she went, and as dusk fell, she kept on a-leaping and a-twirling, till her feet did bleed. At last, she tumbled down and slept right there on the cobbles. Her husband, mighty relieved he was, hoisted her back inside and went to bed, hoping the morrow would forget the madness. But come morn, her side of the bed's empty and there she is again, dancing in the street as if she couldn't stop, with more townsfolk watching, all worried-like.

This dance, it had no cheer to it, the people said. Seemed like the devil himself had got in her. Her eyes did roll back, her mouth a-frothing, and she'd groan and cry out. Once or twice she came to herself for a moment, and she'd plead for saving. Made the blood run cold, they said.

She was a-dancing for five days 'fore her kin took it upon themselves to cart her off to a chapel in the fields, hoping she'd come back to her senses. But as soon as she was out the city gates, word spread of another taken with this terrible torment. And by the next day, three more. All's been in a right tizzy over it, they have. Specially on account of that report what's happening, that is.

Anyway, ain't none of my affair. I'm just here serving pastries. Care for another?

*

By the time the Ammeister's special council convened in the cavernous chamber that afternoon, more than 20 dancers were strutting their stuff on the streets of Strasbourg.

The Ammeister welcomed the XXI, an elite gathering of ministers who run the city.*

### Minutes from part of the XXI council meeting

*(The Minister for the Skies stands up and addresses the chamber)*

MINISTER FOR THE SKIES: Had ministers read my memo on this week's astrological charts, they would be aware the Earth has entered into the 20th degree of the Virgin in opposition to the head of Medusa. Mars and Capricorn are in ascendant. There has never been a more foreboding night sky. We are headed for disaster, gentlemen!

*(Loud jeers. The Minister for Women lurches to his feet)*

MINISTER FOR WOMEN: Be that as it may, my honorable friend, I posit that this began closer to home. This was all started by a woman, was it not? And most of those now dancing are reported to be women. Dare I make a suggestion to the house and ask them to consider that this is nothing more than a pernicious prank, orches-

---

*In 1518, Strasbourg was governed by a council of "ministers," composed of influential burghers (merchants) and appointed magistrates.

trated and enacted by the weaker sex to goad and irritate their husbands!

*(Enthusiastic cheering)*

SPEAKER OF THE HOUSE: Order, order!

MINISTER FOR HEALTH: My honorable friends, I don't think there can be any doubt the afflicted are dancing involuntarily. To dance yourself to exhaustion and bloody your feet in the process is no sensible way to get back at your spouse.

MINISTER FOR WOMEN *(remaining seated)*: That's women for you!

MINISTER FOR GRACE AND VIRTUE: Ministers, is there anything more base, more animal, more perverted than dancing? It is the very essence of sin! I have seen for myself the unholy women in the brothels—through the window—thrusting and gyrating like lustful devils, and I suspect the movements of these degenerates are no different. It is plain to see that God has taken the physical manifestation of their wickedness and cursed them to perform it in perpetuity, as a symbol of their depravity and a warning to all!

*(Hearty grunts of assent)*

MINISTER FOR HEALTH: Ammeister, as convincing as my honorable friend's theory may sound, can he answer why among the women afflicted, none are prostitutes?

MINISTER FOR WOMEN *(yelling, seated)*: All women are prostitutes!

*(Cheers)*

SPEAKER OF THE HOUSE: Order!

MINISTER FOR HEALTH: On the contrary, all confirmed female victims are laborers' wives, servants and old ladies. And what of the men? Are they fellating fornicators too?

MINISTER FOR WOMEN *(mumbling, seated)*: Don't be absurd!

MINISTER FOR HEALTH: May I suggest another cause, Ammeister? After your visit this morning, I took the initiative of tasking a team of physicians to actually visit and assess some of the afflicted.

*(Minister for Health brings out a document)*

They suspect we're dealing with the age-old issue of overheated blood brought on by imbalanced humors. Imbalanced humors caused, of course, by prolonged sinful living.*

Perhaps if the Minister for Grace and Virtue had spent

---

*Despite the technological advancements of the Renaissance, in the 1500s medicine was still dominated by the "humoral theory" favored by the Ancient Greeks, which focused on the four bodily fluids (humors): blood, phlegm, yellow bile and black bile. An imbalance of these could cause all manner of physical and mental ailments. Too much blood could lead to merriment, while hot blood could lead to mad, erratic behavior such as nonstop dancing or dissolving the monasteries.

more time doing his job educating the masses, and less time frequenting brothels, we wouldn't be in this mess.

(*Jeers and laughter*)

MINISTER FOR GRACE AND VIRTUE: Oh f—k off!

SPEAKER OF THE HOUSE: Order, order!

AMMEISTER: My honorable friend, what sort of treatment would you recommend in this case?

MINISTER FOR HEALTH: Ammeister, allow me to defer to my Chief Physician.

CHIEF PHYSICIAN: There is no intervention necessary, Ammeister. I advise we simply allow the dancers to go on dancing. The overheated blood will cool as they perspire, thus solving the problem. Once the blood has cooled, steps can be taken to address the root cause to avoid relapse.

★

After the council meeting, the Minister for Health and his Chief Physician joined Ammeister Andreas for wine in his office.

### Minutes from the meeting between Ammeister Andreas, the Minister for Health and the Chief Physician

AMMEISTER: So we're sure about this hot blood thing, yeah?

MINISTER FOR HEALTH: It's the most plausible explanation.

*(Chief Physician nods)*

MINISTER FOR HEALTH: The bishop sees no reason to pursue spiritual treatment.

AMMEISTER: Right, and there's no medicine for it?

CHIEF PHYSICIAN: Having them dance it off is truly the best treatment.

*(The Ammeister stands up and looks out of the window)*

AMMEISTER: God, I hate dancing.

MINISTER FOR HEALTH: It's just for a few days, Ammeister. Then they'll tire out and everything will go back to normal.

AMMEISTER *(sighs)*: Very well. Let them dance.

★

I took a walk through the city to see the dancers for myself. I counted 33 in total, all flapping away in streets and alleyways, each one commanding the attention of their own little audience. There was no music, just the dull thumps and scrapes of worn-out shoes and the guttural groans of their weary wearers.

Occasionally a distraught relative of one of the afflicted would suspend their stunned silence to call out to their loved one, perhaps sensing a brief lapse in their terrible trance. But the desperate pleas always fell on deaf ears. The dancers kept dancing until they collapsed, at which point they were dragged away to rest. They'd either sleep for a while and then get back up to dance, or never get up again.

As I settled into bed that night, I was inordinately maddened, on account of the long day, to find an old man prancing around on the cobbles beneath my window. Whipped into a frenzy by his incessant, noisy stomps, I took the nearest object—my bedside Bible—flung open the window and launched it in his general direction. Regrettably, rather than scare him away, it hit him square in the head. He staggered into the bushes, where he no doubt slept it off, for he was nowhere to be seen the following morning. I would, of course, never normally use a Bible as a projectile, but in this case, it was clear the poor soul required immediate religious intervention.

*Memo from the Ammeister to the XXI,*
*dated Friday 26 July*

Members of the XXI Council,

As you are all aware, the dancers grow in number every day. Fifty at the last count, and doubtless more by the end of the day. It seems that perspiring away overheated blood is a more protracted process than first anticipated. I have therefore instructed the carpenters' and tanners' guildhalls be emptied and temporarily turned into dance halls so the afflicted may move about in safety. I anticipate everything being back to normal by Monday.

Have a great weekend.
Ammeister Andreas Drachenfels

## *Saturday 27 July*

With no council gatherings or private meetings scheduled, I decided to conduct an inspection of the newly converted dance halls and found both to be at full capacity. Furthermore, the grain market, an additional location cleared for use just that morning, was already getting busy, and set to be packed to the rafters by sundown.

I was about to leave on account of the dreadful peasant stench, exacerbated by the stifling heat, when I noticed a distraught husband and wife depositing an infected old lady at the entrance of the grain market. Watching her galumph inside, the wife burst into tears and buried her head in her husband's chest.

I approached with my Vatican card and, keeping a safe distance, collected a witness statement.

### *Witness statement from the adult son-in-law of an infected old lady*

Well, a gloom had settled upon us after Mary's father took to dancing some nights past, fell a-tumble into the bushes and vanished off the face of the Earth. Yet we pressed on, for what else is to be done, and had just gathered 'round for our midday meal when Mary's mother's ways turned all peculiar-like. At first, we thought 'tis the sorrow for her missing husband taking its toll, but then, quite without her knowing, her shoulders started a-shimmying right there at the table. Well, one thing leads to another, as it tends to do, and next thing we find her grindin' up against the neighbor, doing devilish thrusting and the like, so we had no choice but to bring her here. Me and Mary, we're fair terrified to even move, lest our limbs start doin' their own jig and we're off dancin' too.

*(The witness notices his hands moving in an arc over his head and screams. They come down shaking. Jazz hands.)*

## Monday 29 July

On the Monday morning, while making my way to a council meeting, I ran into the Minister for Health, elbowing his way through a baying mob.

### Minutes from the unscheduled meeting between the Minister for Health and the baying mob

PEASANT: When are you going to do something about the spread, Minister? Nothing is being done to stop the spread!

MINISTER FOR HEALTH: As I have made clear many times, the dance is *not* contagious. It is caused by overheated blood which must be cooled through prolonged perspiration.

PEASANT: You don't have a plan, do you, Minister?

MINISTER FOR HEALTH: We have a very good and sensible plan. It is a full and very nice plan. Every day we're opening more dance spaces in which the sick can dance themselves back to full health as prescribed by the city's physicians.

PEASANT: And what do you say to the families of those who didn't dance themselves back to full health? The ones who danced themselves to death?

MINISTER FOR HEALTH: Look, I extend my most sincere condolences but the science is the science. The science is there, and we have to follow the science. You have to remember that the people dancing are sick people. Their sinful ways have knocked their humors out of balance and now they are paying the price.

PEASANT: Oh, so it's their fault?

MINISTER FOR HEALTH: Look, the science is there and that's all I'll say. The science is there.

PEASANT: Have you ever sinned, Minister?

MINISTER FOR HEALTH: What's important here is that we've got a clear plan and the—

PEASANT: Are you worried you might start dancing too? What with all the grain you've been stockpiling to sell back to us at grossly inflated rates?

MINISTER: Look, I'm aware people are upset but it's important to—

PEASANT: Or maybe you're feeling guilty about capitalizing on the failed harvest by facilitating extortionate loans to farmers who can't pay them back?

MINISTER FOR HEALTH: Right, that's enough questions. Thank you everyone!

*(The minister receives a rotten tomato to the face)*

*

Inside the town hall, I caught Ammeister Andreas marching toward his office followed hurriedly by the Minister for the Skies.

### Minutes from the unscheduled meeting
### between Ammeister Andreas and the Minister for the Skies

MINISTER FOR THE SKIES: Sorry, Ammeister, I was just wondering if my memo made it to—

AMMEISTER: What is it now?

MINISTER FOR THE SKIES: It's just the alignment of Saturn is not exactly ideal, sir . . .

AMMEISTER: Right, can you move it?

MINISTER FOR THE SKIES *(nervous laughter)*: Well, no, but—

AMMEISTER: F—k off then!

*(The Minister for Health appears, shoving the Minister for the Skies out of the way and falling into step with the Ammeister)*

MINISTER FOR HEALTH *(offering the Ammeister a document)*: Some new findings from the physicians, Ammeister.

AMMEISTER *(refusing to take it)*: Break it down for me.

MINISTER FOR HEALTH: Well, the physicians believe our limited success with the "Dance It Out" campaign is due to the dancers taking breaks.

AMMEISTER: . . . Go on.

MINISTER FOR HEALTH: You see, the average dancer goes on for about eight hours before falling down and sleeping. Once they've rested, they get back up and carry on.

AMMEISTER *(visibly frustrated)*: What's your point?

MINISTER FOR HEALTH: Well, the physicians feel that these pauses could actually be counterproductive. When the dancers rest they let the blood resettle and heat back up, undoing all their hard work. One nap and they're back to square one, never actually getting past the necessary threshold to expel the excess heat!

AMMEISTER *(snatching the document)*: Give me that!

MINISTER FOR HEALTH: It all adds up. And it would explain the low recovery rate.

AMMEISTER: How certain are we?

MINISTER FOR HEALTH: All the physicians agree. If the sick are to have a shot at getting rid of their hot blood, they must dance non-stop, with no breaks, until the optimum blood temperature is achieved.

## Minutes from part of the XXI council meeting

AMMEISTER: In light of this new knowledge, conveyed to me by the honorable gentleman on my right, I am releasing funds to hire 20 professional musicians to be stationed at all dance locations. Their continuous playing will encourage flagging dancers to keep moving, no matter how tired they get.

MINISTER FOR STRONG MEN: Ammeister, may I suggest strong men be hired to chaperone the dancers? Music or not, they will grow weary and eventually collapse. With 30–40 strong men on hand, we can ensure the dancers stay upright even when their legs fail them. With your permission I can assemble a small army of strapping lads by sundown.

AMMEISTER: Permission granted! An excellent idea. Minister for Refreshments, is there enough in our stores to give sustenance to the sick? To keep them from exhaustion?

MINISTER FOR REFRESHMENTS (mouth full): Stores are danger-ously low, Ammeister. The best I could offer at this time is half a piece of bread and one cup of weak ale per dancer, per day.

AMMEISTER: It will have to do.

MINISTER FOR REFRESHMENTS: May I suggest sustenance only be provided for dancers entering their second full day of movement, to discourage beggars from faking it for freebies?

AMMEISTER: Very well. We will station personnel at each location to keep a detailed record of all dancers and their comings and goings. Roll call will be made every morning.

MINISTER FOR RECORDERS: Ammeister, regarding the music, may I inquire as to what instruments are to be used?

AMMEISTER *(reading from a list)*: As of now, tambourines, drums, pipes, horns and fiddles.

*(Minister for Fiddles pumps his fist)*

MINISTER FOR RECORDERS: May I suggest one or two re—

AMMEISTER: No further instruments are required at this time.

MINISTER FOR RECORDERS: Understood.

MINISTER FOR CARPENTERS AND TANNERS: Ammeister, may I ask what is to be done about the halls? We are well past full capacity and more and more dancers are arriving every day.

MINISTER FOR GRAINS: The grain market is also at full capacity, Ammeister.

AMMEISTER: Worry not, ministers. My honorable friend the Minister for Edible Animals has agreed to open up the outdoor livestock market to lighten the load. Dancers will be split evenly between all four locations.

MINISTER FOR RECORDERS: Ammeister, if I may be so bold, I would highly recommend the reco—

AMMEISTER: Council adjourned!*

★

Outside, the Ammeister was cornered by the Minister for Construction, who lobbied for a stage to be built on the site of the livestock market.

"To elevate things a little. Make it proper," he said. His brother owned an excellent carpentry firm, apparently, and would do the job for a really good price.

## Wednesday 31 July

The stage was completed within two days and on opening night, wooden boards strained under the weight of a hundred heavy feet. Every few minutes a new dancer would be led up by a teary family member, desperate to see their loved one free from their torment.

"They're lying to us!" one of the mothers said to me as we

---

*Again, this might seem too ludicrous to be true, but there are lots of contemporaneous documents which attest to the rulers of Strasbourg refitting the city's guildhalls, building stages and hiring musicians and chaperones in an effort to help the sick dance away their mania.

watched. "It's not hot blood! It's a curse. A terrible, terrible curse!" I smiled politely and stepped away, removing myself from her onslaught of spittle.

The sounds weren't so awful now. The heavy clomps and scrapes were drowned out by the lively music, a relentless beat that quickened whenever the dancers seemed to tire.

Every so often a sickening thud would break through it all. A lifeless body finally giving up. But it was the brief pauses in the music, when the players stopped to catch their breaths that, ironically, made my blood run cold. It was like pressing my ear against the gates of hell, where a million damned souls writhed within.

I passed the guilds of carpenters and tanners on my way home and popped my head inside their humid, stinking halls. They were both overflowing now. Worried relatives, or at least those who hadn't given up and gone home, crowded around the entrances, praying for a miracle. I stood with them and listened to the rhythmic thump of the drums and tambourines, at the sprightly climbs and falls of the pipes and the energizing plucks of the fiddles. One of the women standing next to me was terrified to notice her foot tapping along to the beat, all on its own. Before she could alert her husband, she was chasséing into the hall and gyrating with the rest of them.

## Saturday 3 August

I arrived early at the town hall to find the Ammeister in an especially foul mood. Three of his servants had not turned up to work, he said, leaving him without breakfast, if I could believe it. His stomach grumbled as the Minister for Graphs ran him through the latest numbers.

### Minutes from the meeting between Ammeister Andreas and the Minister for Graphs

MINISTER FOR GRAPHS: Ammeister, as you can see in this graph, since the construction of the stage and the implementation of music, the numbers have skyrocketed. Before we were looking at five new dancers a day, now it's more like 20.

AMMEISTER: GET ME THE MINISTER FOR HEALTH!

*(The Minister for Graphs drops his documents and scurries away. The Ammeister waits, stewing)*

*(The Minister for Health finally arrives, eyes on the floor)*

MINISTER FOR HEALTH: You called for me, Ammeister?

AMMEISTER *(pointing to the dropped graph)*: What the f—k is this?

MINISTER FOR HEALTH: Well, Ammeister, unfortunately, well, it would seem that—

AMMEISTER: Spit it out!

MINISTER FOR HEALTH: Well, the physicians are thinking it isn't out of the realms of possibility that the dance could be, well . . . infectious.

AMMEISTER: Oh you have got to be F—KING kidding me?!

MINISTER FOR HEALTH *(close to tears)*: It's a slight, small, tiny possibility that, with the introduction of catchy music and with the very public, very visible dancing stage, that healthy onlookers are, well, succumbing.

AMMEISTER: I thought it was hot blood! YOU said it was hot blood!

MINISTER FOR HEALTH: It is! 100 percent. No doubt about it. The physicians believe the onlookers catching it likely already have warmer-than-average blood, and the intoxicating rhythm of the music and the hypnotizing sight of the other dancers excites their already warm blood and makes it hot. Once their blood is hot it's only a matter of time before they start dancing. If you'll just let me fetch the Chief Physician, I'm sure he will be able to . . . because this is not really my . . . it's more them who—

AMMEISTER: Just so we're clear. You're telling me the music and public dancing has only made things worse?

MINISTER FOR HEALTH: Well, it was, y'know, it was an avenue that needed to be explored, but, yes, on current science—

AMMEISTER: Remind me whose idea it was?

MINISTER FOR HEALTH: Well, I was simply going off the physicians, it's the physicians who are the ones who . . . and it's because, y'know, the science available at the time said that—

AMMEISTER: You know someone's head is going to have to roll for this?

MINISTER FOR HEALTH: Well, I . . . I think that—

AMMEISTER: This is a f—k-off-and-never-be-seen-again kind of f—k-up.

MINISTER FOR HEALTH: Per-per-perhaps . . . the Chief Physician?

AMMEISTER: No. A big head. Needs to be a big head.

*(The Minister for Health shrieks and scuttles away clutching his big head)*

## Memo from the Ammeister to the XXI, dated Saturday 3 August

Members of the XXI Council, I have only very recently been made aware that this dreadful dancing plague is contagious. It seems the very sight, sound or suggestion of dancing can induce those susceptible to join in.

We will be drawing up plans for phase two of our approach. In the meantime, panic not. If your conscience is clear, you are safe. The plague seems only to infect the wicked. Those with warm to hot blood who have led lives of vice and sin.

★

A long line of ministers soon formed outside the cathedral, all hoping to be administered an emergency indulgence. There was limited supply, according to a sign outside, and only the most vulnerable were eligible. I had, of course, done nothing wrong, but jumped in the queue just to be safe.

Inside, a team of clergymen heard the babbling confessions of the frightened ministers and unquestionably absolved them, though not before collecting their substantial fee.

I handed over a voucher and, after a short argument about its validity, asked for the comprehensive absolution package to catch any minor sins I was not aware of. In the station next to me, the Minister for Grace and Virtue reeled off the most enormous rap sheet. Forgiven for it all, he skipped off wearing an "I've been forgiven" sticker, as pure and innocent as the virgin mother herself.

The XXI council assembled that afternoon, four ministers short. The Ministers for Knives and Forks, Construction and Topiary, and the former Minister for Health were nowhere to be seen.

### *Minutes from part of the XXI council meeting*

*(Nervous gossip reaches fever pitch)*

AMMEISTER: Ministers! Please settle down. Everything is under control. The "Dance Out to Help Out" campaign has been a resounding success. However, on consulting with the new Minister for Health here—

*(The former Minister for Recorders shifts uneasily in his new seat)*

—and his team of physicians, I've decided to enact phase two of our two-pronged plan. I shall now defer to the honorable gentlemen on my right to talk through the details.

NEW MINISTER FOR HEALTH *(sweating profusely)*: Thank you, Ammeister. Ministers, today the Minister for Graphs revealed a terrifying spike in dancing infections and despite assurances from the former Minister for Health, it has become clear that public dancing is influencing susceptible but not yet infected persons to join in. What's more, the stimulating music being played for the sick—

*(Everyone glares at the Ministers for Drums, Tambourines, Pipes and Fiddles)*

—is only exciting them further. I am therefore, in my first act as Minister for Health, launching a new directive: "Dance IN to WIN." From 6 pm today, any and all dancing *must* take place indoors. Infected persons may dance inside their guilds if they have one, otherwise they must stay at home.

\*

The following notice was nailed to doors and walls across the city:

DANCE IN TO WIN!

Please help stop the spread of the dancing plague.

If you have been infected, you *must* stay at home

or in your guildhall.

If a family member or someone you live with shows symptoms
of the dancing plague (e.g., tapping foot, loose hips, a compulsion
to wiggle the buttocks), you must self-isolate for five days
or until symptoms subside. Until 30 September, all music
and all non-infected dancing (for festivals, weddings or
celebrations) is banned. Violators will incur a 30-shilling fine.
Thank you for doing your bit to stop the spread.

A separate note was sent out to the city's nobles letting
them know that gentle music made by stringed instruments
was still permitted if "absolutely necessary," although any
form of dancing was strongly discouraged.

In the interests of the safety of His Holiness the Pope and
the citizens of Rome, I took the precaution of cancelling my
arranged carriage home. I resolved to remain in Strasbourg
until the dancing plague was over, in case there was any chance
I could spread the disease asymptomatically.

After sending letters to the Vatican and my mother, I
strolled down to the livestock market and watched as the last
stubborn dancers were dragged away. Workers were already
dismantling the stage, ripping out nails and carrying off the
blood-soaked boards into nearby storehouses.

Infected butchers, bakers and candlestick makers were escorted to their respective guilds, who were now obliged to take
them in. Members of the carpenters' and tanners' guilds were
turned away, their halls already at full capacity. For these individuals, and for those unfortunate enough to be guildless, it
was home time. Weary families disappeared into their houses
to endure their relative's incessant stomping for the foresee-
able future.

As the sun set and an ominous gloom descended upon the

hot and sticky city, I weaved through the quiet streets toward my lodgings and passed the Two Step, a small tavern with adjoining brothel, not frequented by the higher classes. Inside the stinking hovel, a dozen or so poor unfortunate souls drank away their sorrows. I decided to enter to gather information on the common people, but immediately aroused suspicion with my fancy trousers and nose clip.

Diffusing the situation by buying a round of drinks for the punters, I set about collecting a series of witness statements.

### Witness statement from a drunk old man

'Tis a plot, I'm tellin' ye. Caught wind of a tale, I did—

*(Interrupted by a series of burps)*

Them dancers, nothin' but puppets of the highborn *(burp)*, set loose to *(burp)* blind us from the *(burp)* true happenings. *(Several burps)* This whole caper's been strung up by Big Gentry *(burp)*, I swear it.

*(Exits to vomit)*

### Witness statement from a lady with enormous breasts

Meself, I trust in the ministers . . . It's the fevered blood, see . . . *(something, something)* . . . and there's me thinkings on the matter.

*(Or thereabouts, the noise made it difficult to concentrate)*

### Witness statement from the landlady

Nay, ye see, this talk of fevered blood's their trick to lay the blame at our feet, when 'tis them that's brewed this storm.

How can we hope for the Lord's grace when our so-called holy men are cavorting with harlots, peddling pardons, and gorging on flesh and wine while we scrape by on scraps? They're supposed to stand for us, be our path to the heavens! Yet, they've let us down, and now St. Vitus, he's raining his fury upon us. 'Tis St. Vitus's curse upon us, and he alone holds the power to lift it!

I stayed to try and extract more information from the lady with enormous breasts and left a short while after.

On my way home, I saw the first 30-shilling fine administered. The man insisted he had simply tripped on a cobblestone and accidentally done a demi-plié, but the warden wasn't having any of it.

## Monday 5 August

On the Monday I woke up to the following note pushed under the door of my apartment:

> You are cordially invited to celebrate the birthday of Ammeister Andreas at a responsible gathering on Wednesday.
>
> Yours,
> Office of the Ammeister

Later that morning, after stopping briefly at the cathedral, I found the town hall teeming. Ministers pulled each other aside for private meetings to plan, plot and gossip. No one was talking about hot blood any more. Apart from a few stubborn physicians, everyone seemed to agree the dancing plague was divine intervention, a direct punishment sent from the heavens to punish wicked individuals down here on Earth.

At midday, all the members of the XXI council gathered for a presentation in Conference Room 3.

### Minutes from part of the presentation conducted by the Minister for Saints

MINISTER FOR SAINTS: So, who was St. Vitus? Anyone?*

*(All ministers seated with their arms crossed)*

MINISTER FOR SAINTS: No? That's okay. *(Nervous laughter)* Well, I'll tell you. St. Vitus was a young martyr, tortured by the Roman emperor in 303 CE for refusing to renounce his faith. Next slide.

*(A servant tears a large sheet of paper from the wall, revealing a new one behind it)*

They put him in a big cauldron of burning tar and lead to teach him a lesson—ouch!—but he climbed out completely unharmed. Next slide.

---

*Saints occupied a prominent position in the minds of medieval Europe. It was widely believed they could inflict illness, cure the sick and curse those who angered them. The Sicilian martyr St. Vitus liked to make his victims dance for their sins. By 1518, a shrine dedicated to the saint, manned by a resident hermit in a cave above nearby Saverne, had become a thriving pilgrimage destination.

The emperor then set a hungry lion on him, but instead of ripping him to shreds, the beast gently licked his hands. Spooky, right? Next slide.

Eventually the young man was allowed to die and go to heaven. But ever since, he has been working his magic here on Earth, cursing and curing whenever and whoever he sees fit, depending on how he's feeling on the day. Next slide.

Amazingly, and we've got the archivists in Cologne to thank for this one, we now know that several minor involuntary dancing incidents have occurred in this country over the last few centuries, if you can believe it.* And guess who they all cited as the saint responsible . . . ?

*(The Minister for Saints makes an impatient signal to the servant, who tears down the penultimate piece of paper. A large drawing of St. Vitus takes up the entirety of the last slide)*

Ta-da!

*

By mid-afternoon, the previously neglected saint's name was on everyone's lips, and ministers gathered in their cliques to share their ideas for quelling his ferocious anger.

The Minister for Grace and Virtue, hitherto brushed aside, now swanned through the corridors wearing a permanent

---

*The previous few centuries had seen at least seven outbreaks of dancing mania in various parts of western Europe, including in 1374 when thousands of men and women across what is now western Germany, the Low Countries and northeastern France were compelled to dance, screech and leap in the air while calling for the mercy of God and the saints.

smirk. He did loops, making it look as though he was always rushing someplace, and batted away the ladder-climbing ministers who yapped at his heels.

Inside the council chamber, the XXI regrouped. The new Minister for Health sulked in the shadows of the back bench, no longer sitting beside the Ammeister. In his place, the Minister for Grace and Virtue served smug looks at his enemies below.

## Minutes from part of the XXI council meeting

AMMEISTER: Ministers, I'm afraid I have been misled by my advisers. As I personally suspected all along, the scientists and physicians of Strasbourg are ill equipped to deal with this terrible predicament. Our people have been struck down by St. Vitus for their sins and indiscretions, and we must now look to make amends on their behalf. We will be drawing up a full and detailed plan over the next few days, but in the meantime, I shall defer to my honorable friend, the Minister for Grace and Virtue, to outline first steps.

*(Jeers)*

MINISTER FOR GRACE AND VIRTUE: Thank you, Ammeister. Yes, as I pointed out from the very start, the wicked people of Strasbourg have inflicted upon themselves a terrible curse. It breaks my heart to see our poor peasants in such turmoil, however just their punishment might be. In order to set the foundation for a full cleanse of the city, I am hereby implementing a temporary banishment of all loose peoples. Gamblers, reprobates, drunkards and the least attractive prostitutes will be sniffed out and sent beyond our walls.

There they shall remain in exile until God's favor is restored, which I estimate will be around 25 September.

*(Cheers and applause)*

## *Tuesday 6 August*

In the morning, I went up to the city gates to watch the sorry procession of scoundrels begin their exile. Only a few of them were infected, leaping and spinning as they went. The rest trudged stoically and collected the following flyer as they left:

SO YOU'VE BEEN EXILED!
If you are reading this, you have been
a very naughty boy / girl.
In light of your deplorable sins, you have been
temporarily banished from Strasbourg by order
of the Ammeister. Use this time to reflect on your life choices
and make amends.
Please do NOT attempt to re-enter the city
until 25 September under any circumstances.
Best of luck and see you soon!
*(If you would like to fast-track your rehabilitation,
consider donating all your money to officials stationed
at the city gates)*

## *Wednesday 7 August*

I arrived at Ammeister Andreas's residence late in the evening, bringing with me a bottle of nice Roman wine and another gift-wrapped indulgence voucher.

On entering, it was clear the Sangiovese was not needed. Gallons of fine wine were being poured by dutiful servants doing the rounds. The indulgence voucher was perhaps slightly more appropriate. All about the sprawling apartments, ministers, merchants and clergymen flirted with beautiful women for hire. I watched as the Minister for Grace and Virtue slipped a few shillings into a dainty hand and was led off behind some curtains, grinning.

The Minister for Women was sitting nearby with an almighty scowl on his face. He recrossed his arms and sighed, so that I might hear him.

"Not much talent tonight, is there?" he grumbled. I nodded and collected a large glass of wine from a passing serving boy.

"I only go for the really fit ones," said the minister, hoping I would agree. I downed the blood of Christ and pushed through throngs of drunken revelers toward the rhythmic thump of a drum. Fiddles followed, and then the bright jingle of tiny tambourine cymbals.

I turned a corner and found myself in the center of the party. All of the ministers were there, drinking, cavorting, groping and dancing. Ammeister Andreas, returning from what looked like a well-received, choreographed routine, stumbled into a side room with a buxom lady under his arm. As he did so, the Minister for Grace and Virtue appeared with his woman and proceeded to drunkenly thrust and gyrate on the dance floor.

I felt an overwhelming desire to leave, but in the interests of bearing witness to all the goings-on in this city, no matter how depraved, I stayed and took another glass of Christ's blood to ease my troubled soul.

After one more glass, I was sufficiently relaxed. So relaxed in fact I felt comfortable enough to collect a witness statement from one of the beautiful women behind the curtains. Unfortunately, I forgot my pen, and was unable to transcribe our brief interaction.

## Thursday 8 August

Nine ministers were missing at the council meeting the following morning. The ones who did make it clutched their throbbing heads and dozed their way through proceedings. I hovered by the door as, for reasons unclear, I was feeling rather queasy.

The Ammeister instructed his aides to check on the no-shows and, desperate for some fresh air, I slipped out of the chamber to join them.

We found the Minister for Women two-stepping in the livestock market, the Minister for Wheelbarrows in a conga line across the town square and the Minister for the Skies doing the worm outside his front door. Three more were found spinning around their living rooms, hopelessly lost in the dreaded trance. The others were fine, they'd just had a lie-in.

The Ministers for Wheelbarrows and Women were hastily escorted home and hidden away, but the townsfolk were already talking. By mid-afternoon, news of the Ammeister's secret party had made its way around half of Strasbourg, and the people weren't happy.

It was around this time I remembered I had neglected to do my bedtime prayers the previous evening, which is a sin of course, and so I headed to the cathedral for an emergency indulgence. As the clergymen reluctantly accepted my voucher and forgave me for my minor indiscretion, the nausea finally subsided. I composed myself and headed back to the town hall where a crowd had formed to chastise ministers as they hurried inside. I squeezed through the crush and received a clump of horse manure to the face.

The XXI assembled in the chamber, the unlucky members still brushing feces off their shoulders. The Minister for Just Deserts, who'd intercepted the worst of it, sat wrapped in an old robe from lost property.

## Minutes from part of the XXI council meeting

MINISTER FOR GRACE AND VIRTUE: Ministers, can you hear the people outside? They are telling us something. They are telling us they've had enough! As shown in the Minister for Graphs' memo this afternoon, after an initial lull in new infections owing to the "Dance IN to WIN" campaign, we're on the upward trajectory again. Hiding the dancers is clearly not enough. They cannot simply dance out their curse. They must be cured!

*(Jeers)*

MINISTER FOR QUESTIONS: But how?

MINISTER FOR GRACE AND VIRTUE: Allow me to welcome into the chamber . . . a common peasant.

*(Loud gasps. Several ministers faint)*

MINISTER FOR GRACE AND VIRTUE: Enter, Frau Troffea.

*(The great doors open and in steps a middle-aged peasant with flushed cheeks and nervous eyes. She walks steadily to the middle of the chamber and plants her feet firmly on the ground)*

MINISTER FOR GRACE AND VIRTUE: My distinguished colleagues, you are looking at St. Vitus's first victim, once locked in a relentless dance, now stood before you, still as a corpse.

*(Disbelieving whispers)*

MINISTER FOR GRACE AND VIRTUE: Tell us, Frau Troffea, how you came to be cured?

FRAU TROFFEA: At Saverne, it was, M'Lord. At the Chapel of St. Vitus. They done Masses and ceremonies, sang songs and chanted spells, and after a few days, there I was, all still and the like, granted mercy at last.

MINISTER FOR GRACE AND VIRTUE: And Frau Troffea is not the only one to have taken the arduous journey to Saverne in search of mercy. Families with the money and means have been carting their loved ones up there since last week. And out of 45 pilgrims, 34 have returned to Strasbourg, completely cured.

*(The ministers turn to each other, amazed. Enthusiastic chatter swells. Applause soon follows. Ammeister Andreas leans over to the*

*Minister for Grace and Virtue and squeezes his shoulder. The Minister for Grace and Virtue sits back down and tries his best to hide his delight)*

## Friday 16 August

It was the Ammeister's wish that all dancers travel to Saverne as soon as possible, but after a week of back-to-back meetings, the plan was looking less and less viable.

It was a 30-mile journey to the remote town and, from there, an afternoon's hike up a steep, craggy mountain to the chapel. A grueling trek for an able-bodied person, an almost impossible one for someone with no control of their limbs. They were going to need assistance.

The Minister for Transport, after weeks with nothing much to do, was suddenly swamped. He barked at his aides as a line of eager ministers jostled outside his office.

After much wrangling, proposals were drawn up to construct a fleet of large wagons. These would carry the majority of the infected to Saverne, at which point they would have to continue on foot.

The Minister for Cathedrals, Churches and Chapels was likewise rushed off his feet. It became alarmingly clear that the Chapel of St. Vitus at Saverne was not up to scratch. The long-neglected site was much too small to accommodate the 400 or so people who'd soon be twirling through its doors. The minister fielded quotes from the town's construction firms to build a new, overflow chapel next to the old one. In a remarkable coincidence, his own company submitted the winning proposal.

The costs for the vehicles, construction, priests, personnel and assorted ceremony paraphernalia were totted up and a full report was delivered to the Ammeister.

Once he was done screaming, he called an emergency meeting with the Treasurer.

### Minutes from part of the meeting
### between Ammeister Andreas and the Treasurer

TREASURER: No way! There's just no way.

AMMEISTER: Can we take it from elsewhere? Walls got a lot of money this year.

TREASURER: Now's not the time to be underfunding walls.

AMMEISTER: What about pastries? That big cash injection, can we reverse that?

TREASURER: You'd deny the ministers their pastries? *(Scoffs)* I didn't have you down for a barbarian, Ammeister!

AMMEISTER: There must be something we can skim off!

TREASURER: It's a no can do, I'm afraid.

★

Everyone was tearing their hair out trying to think of ways to siphon a few shillings from their budgets until the Minister for Cathedrals, Churches and Chapels knocked on the Ammeister's door with an idea.

*Minutes from the meeting between Ammeister Andreas
and the Minister for Cathedrals, Churches and Chapels*

MINISTER FOR CATHEDRALS, CHURCHES AND CHAPELS:
What if, instead of going to St. Vitus, we brought St. Vitus to us?

AMMEISTER *(brushing pastry crumbs off his shirt)*: . . . Go on.

MINISTER FOR CATHEDRALS, CHURCHES AND CHAPELS: I
was thinking, perhaps, a huge Mass at the cathedral. We'll go all out,
all the bells and whistles. We'll make a votive, coax down St. Vitus
and with any luck, he'll cure as many people as he can right here in
the city.

AMMEISTER: Would that work?

MINISTER FOR CATHEDRALS, CHURCHES AND CHAPELS: I
see no reason why not. It'd snap some of them out of it, I'm sure. A
big spectacle to rally the city! And those who aren't cured we can
cart off to Saverne at half the price.

★

The Treasurer, who owned a gift shop right next to the cathedral, signed off on the plan right away.

"Money spent *in* the city," he said, "is money well spent."

The Minister for Grace and Virtue was fully on board with
the idea. He felt that an impressive Mass, with hundreds upon
hundreds of people praying for mercy, would almost certainly
attract the attention of the incandescent saint. He did feel,
though, that an expensive offering would seal the deal. The

Ammeister and Treasurer agreed, releasing funds for a huge, 100-pound wax sculpture of St. Vitus sitting in a cauldron of molten tar.

It was decided that any infected guild members needing to travel to Saverne after Mass would have their travel and accommodation paid for by their guilds. The poorest dancers—those unfortunate enough to have no guild affiliation—would be paid for out of the city coffers.

## Saturday 24 August

On the day of the big Mass, every dancer was rounded up and led to the cathedral. Their families joined them, bringing with them little trinkets and offerings for the saint. The centerpiece, the bespoke 100-pound wax sculpture, had been created at great expense, and then melted down into a massive candle after ministers realized it would be too difficult to transport to Saverne in its original form. I suggested to the Treasurer that a considerable amount of money could have been saved if they had just made a candle in the first place, but was told to depart from his presence with the use of an expletive.

The Ammeister and a dozen other ministers attended the Mass. They were led in wearing eye masks, lest they see a dancer and catch the disease so close to the finish line. I purchased a mask from the gift shop and placed it on my head.

The Mass was an auditory overload of praying, singing and weeping. The scrapes and squeaks of restless feet that had filled the cathedral at the beginning of the service softened with each prayer and by the time the bishop wrapped things up, the whole place was promisingly quiet.

Dizzy from the incense, we swayed and stumbled outside, hands on the shoulders of the man in front. We assembled in the courtyard, still blindfolded, and waited for a report from the bishop.

*Minutes from the meeting*
*between Ammeister Andreas and the bishop*

BISHOP: I don't want to speak too soon, Ammeister—

AMMEISTER: Who said that?

BISHOP: It's me, the bishop.

AMMEISTER: Ah! A lovely service, Bishop!

BISHOP: I'm over here, Ammeister.

AMMEISTER: Where?

BISHOP: Here!

AMMEISTER: Oh I see. Give me the numbers, Bishop.

BISHOP: Well, we won't know for sure until we process all the feedback forms, but it looks like we made a dent in it. Those in a lighter trance seemed to make a full recovery. I'd say 100–150 walked out unaided.

AMMEISTER: Not bad. Not bad at all.

BISHOP: I had hoped for more but the rest were just in too deep. I couldn't get through, it seems.

★

The ministers retired as the remaining dancers, some 200 of them, were herded toward the waiting wagons. I took off my blindfold and watched through the gaps in my fingers as hired help loaded them on like cattle, more than a dozen to a vehicle. Limited on space, the more able bodied were made to trail behind in a disorderly procession, family members and personnel making sure they didn't veer off and disappear.

With a sharp cry from the procession leader, the wagon train lurched forward and rolled away. I followed it to the city gates and joined the well-wishers waving goodbye. The bizarre parade snaked along the road and across the fields. The last I saw of it was the Minister for Women doing a pirouette on the crest of the hill. He dipped below the horizon with a flourish, and was gone.

## Thursday 29 August

The subsequent days at the town hall were remarkably quiet. Ministers sat around and waited for news from Saverne, filling their time with idle chitchat and diplomatic visits to the local brothel.

I was having lunch with the Ammeister when word finally arrived.

The procession had reached Saverne the morning after

they'd set out, with only a few dancers lost along the way, condemned to gyrate in forests and fields for the rest of their days. Several collapsed and died on the arduous climb to the chapel and were spared the grueling regime that awaited the survivors.

On arrival, the infected were separated into groups and led before the shrine. There they were each presented with a pair of special red shoes.*

"An essential part of the ritual," the Minister for Grace and Virtue had promised the council. The Treasurer had no choice but to pay a considerable number of shillings to the city's foremost cobbling firm, of which the Minister for Grace and Virtue just so happened to be a majority shareholder.

Wearing their expensive new footwear smudged with oil and balsam in the shape of a cross, the dancers deposited their offerings (a penny) and were sent circling around the altar to begin the purification of their souls. Spirited chants and incantations followed as they choked on the heavy fumes that filled their lungs and singed the hairs in their nostrils. The ceremonies went on for hours, we were told. A relentless ordeal of prayers and devotions, circling and prostrating.

Resting afterward, priests, family members and attendants waited to see who would wake up cured. Those who hadn't done enough to receive absolution were put back in their red shoes and sent again before the angry saint.

Of the 200 or so dancers sent to Saverne, 150 returned within days, completely cured. The rest were left to repeat the

---

*In perhaps the first recorded incidence of retail therapy, the afflicted townspeople of Strasbourg were given red shoes to wear, perhaps to reflect the red flames or fiery torment of St. Vitus. By this point, the townspeople were clearly desperate: red dye was egregiously expensive and normally reserved for the wealthy, and not a peasant doing the tarantella.

ceremony again and again, though with slight experimental changes in the program. Incredibly, five women were cured without the all-important red shoes and one man found forgiveness simply by looking at a painting of St. Vitus and saying, "Sorry, mate."

## Friday 13 September

The newly cured trickled one by one back into the city and by 13 September, aside from a few isolated incidents, the plague had fizzled into oblivion. St. Vitus was appeased and Strasbourg, after two months under a bizarre and crippling curse, was free.

Safe in the knowledge I wasn't endangering anyone by returning home, I packed my things and bade farewell to Ammeister Andreas, thanking him for his extended hospitality. I was only meant to stay for a week but had spent nearly the entire summer locked down in his city.

He thanked me in advance for portraying him and his ministers so favorably in my upcoming report and gifted me a handful of silver tokens to use for procuring "entertainment" on the way home. I gratefully accepted, of course, but for obvious reasons had no use for them.

## Monday 28 October

After a strangely pleasurable journey, I arrived in Rome in good spirits, and set to work compiling my findings. However, on hearing the topline of my incomplete dossier, His Holiness was eager to receive my observations first hand, and summoned me to his chambers immediately.

He listened from his magnificent, bejeweled throne as I told him of St. Vitus's curse, how it had engulfed the city of Strasbourg and stupefied those in charge.

"Jesus Christ!" he said when I was finished. "Is it contagious?"

"Yes, Your Holiness," I replied. "By sight and suggestion, it would seem. But you've no need to be concerned. It only affects the wicked."

I retired to my apartment below the Pope's residence, stripped naked and washed in the basin, giddy with excitement to sleep in my own bed after months away.

I made a quick prayer, thanking the Lord for his love and guidance, and then climbed into bed. I stretched my legs and felt the softness of the silk sheets against my skin, shivering in delight as the goose-down mattress cradled me like an angel's sweet embrace. And then, quite out of nowhere, my toes wiggled, all on their own.

I sat up and stared at them, twitching away, and watched in horror as the spasm crawled into my ankles.

Tap, tap, tap. My feet rapped on the gold-plated bed frame. Tap, tap, tap. The muted promise of an irresistible beat.

Then came the thump from the Pope's residence upstairs. Another one and another one. My chandelier rattled with the rhythm of his feet, and as I looked up at the creaking ceiling, an invisible hand plucked me from my bed and dropped me on the floor.

Naked in the moonlight, my feet fell into time with the holy toes bouncing on the boards above. My hips rocked, my buttocks popped, and for what could have been days or weeks or months, we danced and danced and danced.

## THE FACTS

It might seem like the invention of an insane comedian, but the dancing plague of Strasbourg really did happen, as did the infuriating mismanagement of the whole affair.*

With an exhausted population ravaged by famine and plague, and with religious tensions sweeping across northern Europe, it's perhaps unsurprising the city of Strasbourg fell victim to this strange bout of mass hysteria. Records from the time detail how residents were gripped by an uncontrollable urge to dance, beginning with a woman named Frau Troffea, whose solitary jig in the street turned into a four- to five-day marathon of trance-like twitching. Onlookers assumed a restless spirit, saint or demon had taken hold of her, an affliction which then spread to hundreds of other people who joined in the wild dancing, despite the punishing summer heat.

The extraordinary dance-athon dominated discussions of Strasbourg's ruling Privy Council, all of which were minuted and still survive. In hastily convened meetings, all other matters were swept aside as the Ammeister Andreas Drachenfels and his fellow councillors grappled with how to contain the epidemic, desperately flip-flopping between different strategies.

Frau Troffea began dancing on 14 July, and over the subsequent week 34 others took to the streets, rising to 50 by 25 July. The Privy Council decided first to seek advice from leading physicians, who dismissed the superstitions of the people,

---

*John Waller's book *A Time to Dance, a Time to Die* gives an excellent and thoroughly researched account of the dancing plague and the local government's clumsy handling of it.

blaming the mania instead on overheating or "hot blood." The remedy was to let the afflicted dance it out, which the council facilitated. They cleared halls, erected stages, ordered musicians to play day and night and hired robust men to hold up anyone who flagged or collapsed.

By early August, however, the number of dancers had grown to 100 and it was clear the strategy needed a major rethink. In an about-turn, the council dismantled the stages, dismissed the musicians, issued a ban on dancing and music for two months, and banished all loose persons from the city. (Notably, the dancing ban didn't extend to "honorable persons" who were allowed to jig at certain celebrations to the accompaniment of stringed instruments, avoiding the pulsating rhythm of the tambourine or drum.) By the middle of August, as many as 200 to 400 people were caught up in the dancing mania, finally convincing the Privy Council the dancing had nothing to do with hot blood and more to do with a ticked-off saint.

Orders went out to dispatch dancers not cured by an in-city Mass directly to the St. Vitus shrine at Saverne, where craftsmen had been sent to build a new chapel and altar. Victims were given red shoes to wear and small crosses to hold, before assembling before the shrine and engaging in an exhausting, incense-filled ritual. Gradually the epidemic began to subside and by the end of September prohibitions against public dancing and the playing of drums, horns and tambourines were lifted. Strasbourg's leaders could finally focus on other neglected matters, and the dancing mania—or choreomania—never came back to the city.

Reports of the Pope's succumbing to the plague are unsubstantiated, but as the man at the top of a darkly corrupt institution, he was no doubt anxious about the disquiet bubbling at the far reaches of the empire. Soon, a fed-up priest called Martin Luther would ignite a movement that would shake the foundations of the Catholic Church, leading a revolution against the hypocritical gatekeepers of salvation and (mostly) putting an end to the sale of indulgences. It is not known whether the Minister for Grace and Virtue or the more unscrupulous members of Strasbourg's elite stockpiled any vouchers for a rainy, sinful day.

# 6.

# *The Deputy Groom of the Stool*

King Henry VIII, arguably history's most notorious monarch, was a formidable man. As two of his six wives found out, getting acquainted with the tetchy tyrant was risky business, but it could also be incredibly rewarding.

In Henry's court, few positions were as sought after as the "Groom of the Stool." There to assist the King in the toilet and see to his intimate physiological needs, the groom spent more alone time with the boss than anybody else, enjoying a great deal of influence as a result.

Holding the enviable role between 1536 and 1546, Thomas Heneage's daily log has never been found, but one belonging to his deputy, Anthony Denny, was recently unearthed in a Tudor self-storage facility next to Elizabeth I's spoon collection. While Heneage was in charge of keeping the *official* medical records, for personal reference or posterity, Denny took it upon himself to make his own, complete with private notes and observations.

Below, published here for the first time, are a curated selection of these daily entries.

## DAILY REPORT: 12 September 1539

2 am—Bowel movement: After a bedtime enema, His Majesty awoke to perform a strong and persistent discharge, contents of which were full and firm, indicating complete evacuation. A long and sustained note marked the finish, of which the Royal trumpeter would be proud.*

*(Look into getting sense of smell removed. Surgery?)*

Upon waking at 7 am, His Majesty's indigestion was greatly improved, having spent the better part of yesterday evening in great discomfort.

Mr. Heneage made yet another appeal: "Perhaps only one meat dish at supper, Your Majesty, instead of rabbit, peacock, swan *and* pheasant?" he said. "And mayhaps it's just me, but I've always found that if one sticks to just one glass of wine, one finds the evening considerably more enjoyable."

Mr. Heneage received a thunderous belch to the face.

The King has spent the rest of the day in his usual malaise. It is almost two years since the death of his beloved third wife,

---

*A letter from Thomas Heneage to the King's chief minister Thomas Cromwell describes an enema being administered to Henry. This usually took the form of a pig's bladder filled with a weak solution of salt and infused herbs, which slowly trickled into the King's anus via a greased metal tube. It resulted, as Heneage put it, in "a fair siege."

Jane Seymour.* His persistent grief, burgeoning weight and ailing health makes for a stew of misery and regret.

Mr. Heneage has done his best to perk him up, reminding him that love is just around the corner. The King's most trusted adviser, Thomas Cromwell, is drawing up plans for a marriage with Anne of Cleves, a princess (of sorts) from the lower Rhinelands. His Majesty, however, has been reticent about the proposed union. He is an old romantic at heart and agreeing to marry someone before meeting them is, understandably, making him anxious.

"It's a win-win, sire," said Mr. Heneage as he inspected the Royal hemorrhoids. "An ingenious political alliance, as well as a beautiful new wife."

*(The niece of my old pal, the Duke of Norfolk, knows Anne and, from what I hear, she is not Henry's type at all. She's not anyone's type by all accounts. But Cromwell is all in, and since Heneage usually agrees with whatever Cromwell says, he's all in too. How quickly one forgets the mistakes of one's predecessor! The last groom, poor Henry Norris, was all in for Boleyn . . . until his head rolled off the scaffold after hers)*

4 pm—Attempted bowel movement: Five minutes of aggressive gas, no stool.

*(Can now hold my breath for a full three minutes)*

*Jane Seymour died in October 1537, 12 days after giving birth to Henry's much longed-for male heir, Edward VI, who, it was hoped, would carry on the family name for many years to come. Unfortunately, the future king died at the ripe old age of 15.

. . .

A portrait of Anne was commissioned some months ago and the King is impatient to see it. He had previously sent envoys to "check on the talent" but they, for whatever reason, were refused a look at the mysterious woman.

"I'm only going through with it if she's fit," he remarked as I rubbed special ointment on his groin ulcers.

"May I be so bold, sire . . . " I said, making sure Mr. Heneage was out of earshot, "to suggest you meet her first, before agreeing to anything?"

The King squinted.

"The portrait will do," he said, releasing a steady stream of wind.

Summary of today's treatments:

3:45 pm: Experimental rectal flushing with live eels (abandoned)
6:30 pm: Hemorrhoid mask with rhubarb pulp
9:30 pm: Special ointment applied to ulcers

King's bedtime mood:
☹

## DAILY REPORT: *30 September 1539*

His Majesty spent the morning pacing (limping) up and down, deeply anxious about the imminent arrival of Anne of Cleves's portrait.

9 am—Attempted bowel movement: Almost there, but proceedings had to be cut short due to uncompliant sitter.

"What's the rhyme that's going about? The one no one will tell me?" asked the King. Mr. Heneage looked at me and shook his head.

"It's: 'Divorced, beheaded, died—try your luck as Henry's bride,' sire," I told him blankly. The King stared at me, expressionless, and for a moment I could almost feel the cold edge of an axe on my neck. And then he laughed.

When, after luncheon, the long-awaited portrait of Anne of Cleves finally arrived, we all got a good look at it before bringing it to the King. The artist, Holbein, has painted a radiant creature.* A sweet and delicate beauty. Cromwell and Mr. Heneage are feeling very smug.

"I told you! I told you she was going to be smoking hot!" said Mr. Heneage.

The King became instantly animated upon the unveiling and pumped his fist in excitement.

"Get in there!" he said.

4 pm—Bowel movement: A full and liberating exodus.

As we cleaned up the aftermath, the King instructed Cromwell to bring negotiations to a speedy conclusion.

"I want a marriage treaty on my desk by Wednesday," he barked.

---

*Hans Holbein the Younger was the finest painter of the age whose famed portraits served as a Tudor precursor to internet dating. Every noble in Europe wanted him to do their headshots.

Following nighttime treatments, Mr. Heneage invited me for a drink to celebrate / gloat.

"Sometimes, to win in this life, you just have to put all your eggs in one basket," he purred, bobbling his big head.

Summary of treatments performed:

9 am: Stimulating abdominal massage
9:15 am: Intimate tickling with peppermint leaves
6 pm: Steam bath with oil massage
9 pm: Warm cloth compress to hemorrhoids

King's bedtime mood:
☺

## DAILY REPORT: 4 October 1539

The persistent melancholy of the last few months seems to have subsided, leaving the King in good spirits.

9 am—Bowel movement: A lengthy parade of all possible forms. Complete evacuation achieved.

I inspected the King's leg ulcers, massaged his head and spritzed him with a new perfume.

*(Apparently no way to surgically remove sense of smell)*

His Majesty signed the marriage treaty after lunch. We're told Anne of Cleves was doing the same over in Düsseldorf. The

King had an attendant pour us all a celebratory glass of wine and took one sip before the privy beckoned.

2 pm—Bowel movement: Protracted but continuous flow, colossal quantities of gas forming a somewhat *legato* melody. The King quite liked the tune and called on the court composer to transcribe. "I shall call it 'Greensleeves,'" he announced proudly.

"I knew she'd be perfect!" said Mr. Heneage at various points throughout the saga. "Didn't I tell you from the start, sire?"

"Denny wanted me to wait until I met her!" said the King.

His Majesty was smiling, but Mr. Heneage shot me a glare that could have cooked a hog roast in seconds.

Outside, I received a strongly worded verbal warning. Giving advice to the King was his job, he said. And to disagree with him and Thomas Cromwell on the subject of the future Queen was tantamount to treason.

"Deputy," he said stabbing my chest with his finger. "Groom," he said, pointing to himself.

"Deputy" to me; "groom" to him. He did this for about four or five rounds before realizing how silly it looked.

Summary of treatments performed:

9:15 am: Special ointment applied to ulcers
9:30 am: Head massage with essential oils
5:45 pm: Woodlouse liver face mask
8:00 pm: Full body manscaping

King's bedtime mood:
☺

## DAILY REPORT: 1 January 1540

This morning Mr. Heneage and I prepared to travel to Rochester Castle to join Anne of Cleves's preliminary welcoming committee. The plan was for her to meet the King at Hampton Court in a few days, after settling in and getting her bearings at Rochester.

His Majesty awoke anxious, eager to lay eyes on his wife-to-be.

> 7 am—Attempted bowel movement: A valiant effort, but nothing.

The King floated the idea of coming with us instead of waiting for the proposed meeting at Hampton Court. I said it was an excellent idea—"incredibly romantic." But Mr. Heneage quickly shut it down.

"Let her settle in, sire," he said. "She'll be tired and disheveled. Best we get her ready and you meet her once she's all freshened up." He tried to hide his nervous eye-twitch, but I saw it jittering away.

The King's bowel movements were left in the care of a temp during our absence.

A welcoming committee assembled outside the front doors of Rochester Castle just after lunch, some 25 of us, including the Duke of Norfolk.

*(Always nice to see the old chap)*

As we waited, Mr. Heneage made a point of flaunting an exquisite new brooch pinned to his hat—"Oh, that?" he said, though I wasn't really looking. "Just a little something from the King, for my good counsel." Thomas Cromwell, likewise, made sure everyone could see his shiny new necklace.

After some time, the convoy of carriages approached and out of one, announced by her valet, stepped the long-awaited Anne of Cleves.

"Oh you have got to be kidding me," mumbled Mr. Heneage.

*(Glorious, glorious!)*

The Duke of Norfolk's niece was right after all, for the lady standing before us was about as radiant as a sack of onions. Her long nose sat in between two dull eyes, roughly assembled on a gray, pallid, pockmarked face. Her clothes were, let's say, functional rather than fashionable, and to top it all off she wore the most hideous hat I've ever seen.★

Just as Mr. Heneage leaned in to remark how lucky we were the King wasn't with us, the King (in disguise) appeared out of nowhere, riding over the hill with a handful of attendants.†

---

★Had Anne known she would be seeing the King, she would undoubtedly have dressed more appropriately. The French ambassador, in an early example of a French person judging someone else's outfit, was recorded as commenting on her "monstrous habit and apparel." Suffice to say, she was not the radiant beauty Henry was expecting.

†The King, the old romantic he was, decided to don a disguise and surprise his future wife. Courtly notions of love dictated that the lady would recognize her betrothed despite the disguise. Anne just thought the whole thing seemed a bit strange.

"Oh you have got to be kidding me," said Cromwell, covering his face.

The attendants helped the King dismount, being careful not to aggravate his ulcers, and brought him before Anne. When he caught his breath, he turned to look at Cromwell and Heneage. Even with his mask on I could detect his almighty frown.

With an impatient hand signal from Cromwell, the King went to kiss his fiancée, but the lady, frightened by the masked man, recoiled.

"*Nein, Schwein!*" she yelped.

The King turned to Cromwell and Heneage.

"Sorry—does someone want to tell me what is going on?!" he bellowed.

"Who are you?" asked the sack of onions.

"WHO ARE *YOU*?!" screamed the King.

5 pm—Bowel movement: Violent diarrhea.

The King has spent the evening incandescent, ranting endlessly to Thomas Cromwell, who organized the whole thing.

"I like her not! I like her not!" he screamed in between apoplectic expulsions of wind.

Mr. Heneage backed into a corner and chewed his fingernails down to the knuckle.

"You caught her on a bad day, sire," said Cromwell.

"Cancel it, I'm not marrying her!"

The King dismissed Heneage and Cromwell and refused his bedtime steam bath and oil massage, but permitted me to apply special ointment to his inflamed ulcers. I worked in silence, the only words exchanged between us spoken as I was leaving.

"F—king Holbein," grumbled His Majesty, gulping down a king-sized wine.

"Indeed," I said, before skipping home.

Summary of treatments performed:

7:00 am: Stimulating abdominal massage
7:15 pm: Experimental ginger elixir applied to perineum
8:30 pm: Genital refresh (with venison bone broth)
10:00 pm: Special ointment applied to ulcers

King's bedtime mood:
☹

## DAILY REPORT: 7 January 1540

Despite the King's reluctance, the wedding went ahead yesterday in Greenwich. Mr. Heneage entered the King's bedchamber this morning expecting to find him with his new wife, but he was alone. I followed shortly after.

8 am—Attempted bowel movement: Ungodly gas, the breath of Lucifer himself.

*(Stick lavender up nostrils?)*

His Majesty was hungover from the wedding feast last night as, I daresay, was I.

He spent the days leading up to the nuptials desperately trying to think of ways to back out, but eventually agreed to go ahead after Thomas Cromwell said it would be political suicide not to.

*(In my mind, His Majesty is quite immune to political suicide, having committed it many times)*

The King is a marvelous actor and played the part of the pleased husband very well, although I'm sure the gallons of wine helped somewhat.* We even had a drunken heart-to-heart, witnessed by an incensed Mr. Heneage. Though I can't remember most of what was said, I do recall the King burping in my ear and slurring, "You're all right, mate, you know—do you know that? Like, don't let anyone, like, you know . . . I've got you. I've got you. You're my bro." He proceeded to vomit in my lap and laugh about it, but the kind words were no less sweet.

"Did you have an eventful night, sire?" asked Mr. Heneage this morning, gesturing to the bed.

The King rolled his eyes and made no effort to answer.

9 am—Attempted bowel movement: No progress.

---

*Despite Henry's misgivings, the wedding between him and Anne went ahead on 6 January 1540, followed by three days of celebrations on Blackheath Common in Greenwich. The pre-planned festivities made for a dazzling spectacle with tents and pavilions sumptuously decorated in gold cloth, the soon-to-be bride and groom bejeweled and bedecked in velvet, gold damask and an assortment of Tudor bling. Publicly, the couple appeared delighted with their impending nuptials, whereas in private the King grumbled to Cromwell and no doubt Heneage and Denny about having to "put my neck in the yoke."

Mr. Heneage prepared an enema for the post-feast constipation but His Majesty refused.

"Denny will do it later," he said. Mr. Heneage shot me a red-hot glare.

The silent treatment wasn't afforded to Thomas Cromwell, who arrived after midday wholly unprepared for the tempest awaiting him.

"So, has the marriage been . . . consummated?" he asked.

"What do you think?! Have you seen her? Or are you blind?"

"I think she is quite beautiful, sire."

"She looks like a wonky horse!" screamed the King.

Mr. Heneage and I guided His Majesty through several breathing exercises, at the end of which he expelled great quantities of wind and eventually calmed down. I considered calling on the court composer to record the dramatic composition, but thought better of it.

"I just couldn't get it up!" admitted His Majesty, finally.

"Perhaps it was the wine?" said Mr. Heneage. The King batted him away, refusing his counsel.

"I looked at every bit of her, searching for something to get me going. But there was nothing. NOTHING!"

We all stood in silence.

"As you well know, I didn't like her before but now I really, *really* don't like her. There's nothing fair about her. And to add insult to injury, she stinks!"*

---

*Surviving accounts give a wealth of detail on Henry's wedding night with Anne of Cleves, suggesting he may already have been laying the groundwork for a swift annulment. Along with his complaints of her "evil smells," the King confirmed, "I have felt her belly and her breasts and thereby as I

12:30 pm—Attempted bowel movement: Sulfurous gas.

We were all dismissed.

Thomas Cromwell invited Mr. Heneage and me for a walk, during which he insisted we do everything we can to see the marriage consummated. Mr. Heneage, ever dutiful, assured Cromwell he would be able to coax the King into coitus. I made no promises.

At dinnertime I had the pleasure of receiving my old friend the Duke of Norfolk, who wished to discuss a confidential matter concerning his niece, Catherine (one of Queen Anne's ladies-in-waiting). We had a productive chat.

Later I was invited back into the Royal bedchamber to tend to the Royal rectum alone. I administered the treatments in silence, until I felt the King's shoulders relax during his head massage.

"Sire?" I said.

"What is it?" replied the King.

"Does the name Catherine Howard mean anything to you?"*

9 pm—Bowel movement: An entire banquet's worth, all at once.

---

can judge she should be no maid." There's often too little historical record to build a good picture of a monarch's intimate moments. In this instance there's too much.

*The Duke of Norfolk had indeed secured a prized position for his niece Catherine Howard as lady-in-waiting to the new Queen. She had, apparently, caught the attention of the King during his first disastrous meeting with Anne of Cleves.

Summary of treatments performed:

8:15 am: Abdominal massage

8:30 am: Cucumber eye mask (reapplied three times because he kept eating them)

9:45 pm: Calming primrose-scented balm applied to buttocks

10:00 pm: Head massage with essential oils

King's bedtime mood:

## DAILY REPORT: 20 April 1540

This morning I tended to His Majesty alone. Mr. Heneage returned from holiday yesterday afternoon, but the King is keen to "spread out responsibilities."

Mr. Heneage confronted me late last night after a skinful of ale and while most of what he said was unintelligible, I gathered he was upset at the "dilution of his position."

9 am—Bowel movement: Free and plentiful.

The King is in good spirits. In direct affront to the recommendations of his once closest adviser Thomas Cromwell, he has tasked ministers with getting him out of his unholy matrimony.

Incidentally, before lunch I received a rather desperate letter from Cromwell instructing me to use my new favor with the King to pour Anne-flavored honey into his ear. He is anxious to get the marriage consummated as soon as possible.

.    .    .

*(But I would* hate *to spoil His Majesty's good mood)*

I administered a rhubarb mask to the King's hemorrhoids before luncheon. He lay face down on the bed and asked for my opinion on the whole situation.

"Well, I would never want to go against Mr. Heneage, him being my boss and all," I said, my hands parting his enormous buttocks. "But I reckon the sooner you can get rid of that horrible woman the better."

"Damn right," said the King. "And don't worry about Heneage. You report to me."

*(Excellent)*

12:00 pm—Bowel movement: Latecomers from the previous deluge.

"I gifted Catherine the land, by the way. And that stack of nice silks you suggested. Sure it's not a bit much?" he said as I massaged his thighs this afternoon.

"She'll be thrilled, sire, I know it."

His Majesty has fallen head over heels for the youthful beauty and, in between bowel movements, wants to do nothing more but woo her.

5:30 pm—Bowel movement: Like a Tudor pie, rich and layered. Science-defying flatulence throughout.

*(Perhaps it's just the lavender shoved up my nose but I swear the King's discharge is smelling sweeter)*

Lovely supper with the Duke of Norfolk after work. He gifted me a very expensive bottle of wine and a manor house in Norwich.

Summary of treatments performed:

11:30 am: Hemorrhoid mask with rhubarb pulp
3:30 pm: Thigh massage with therapeutic wild boar bladder paste
6:00 pm: Steam bath with oil massage
6:30 pm: Special ointment applied to ulcers

King's bedtime mood:
☺

## DAILY REPORT: 9 July 1540

The King had a spring in his step this morning (figuratively speaking, of course—the man can barely walk). Just after breakfast he received confirmation that his marriage with Anne of Cleves had been successfully annulled after much legal wrangling.

9 am—Bowel movement: Like a great dam thrown open.

The King's bad mood now fully abated, Mr. Heneage has managed to slip back into the fold.

"Look, I'll say it, I never liked her," he told the King this morning as we toasted the annulment. "Let her rot!"

The King gave me one of his "can you believe this guy?" looks—which is just the kind of thing we do now.

Mr. Heneage, now not quite as close to the King, hasn't been party to his ever-changing thoughts and opinions. He's unaware that, owing to her compliance in the annulment and for not kicking up a fuss, the King quite likes the sack of onions now (just not in that way). He likes her so much he's given her a palace!

"I think of her like a sister," he told me.*

The King went hunting after lunch and returned to be bathed. Mr. Heneage administered a deep clean of the King's toenails and I saw to his ulcers, which had flared up during the afternoon's activities.

"So, Heneage, what do you think of Catherine?" asked the King. Mr. Heneage looked at me, a quiet panic bubbling up inside of him.

"Well, I think, I suppose I think whatever—whatever you think . . ."

The King rolled his eyes. Heneage noticed.

"I mean, what I think is that she's very lovely."

"Right," said the King.

"But maybe it'd be best to wait . . . before doing anything rash," said Mr. Heneage, finally noticing my magnificent new brooch.

---

*Despite their rocky start, Henry and Anne remained on good terms long after the official annulment of their marriage on 9 July 1540. Henry even awarded Anne the highly honorable, and not at all confusing, position of the King's Sister.

.    .    .

*(Too late, my dear)*

Summary of treatments performed:

11:30 am: Deep clean of Royal crevasse, including anal
   bleaching
4:45 pm: Warm bath with pheasant-lung bath bomb
5:00 pm: Deep clean beneath toenails
5:15 pm: Special ointment applied to ulcers

King's bedtime mood:
☺


## DAILY REPORT: 28 July 1540

The King married Catherine Howard today. He seemed to
float out of bed—all the trials and tribulations of the last few
months a distant memory. Not even his swollen piles or oozing
ulcers could bring him down.

8 am—Bowel movement: One of the best I've ever seen. No
notes.

Mr. Heneage was absent for morning duties, but neither the
King nor I missed his presence. I am now confident in admin-
istering all treatments myself.

I proceeded with a precautionary enema to ensure His Majesty was all flushed out before the big day.

Just as he was filled, a messenger arrived with news from
the Tower. Thomas Cromwell was dead.

"Should I have done that, d'you think?" His Majesty asked when the boy left.

"He all but forced you into a disastrous marriage, sire. Even without the rumors of plotting and rebellion, that is treason enough."

It took three blows of the axe to cut his head off, we were told.

"Probably should've hired a better executioner," said the King.

I sensed his mood taking a turn, the sticky fingers of regret pulling him back toward the suffocating malaise of winter.

"No sire, he deserved it," I said.

9 am—Bowel movement: Like a mountain spring.

Mr. Heneage finally arrived as white as a sheet. He apologized profusely for his tardiness and kept his gaze firmly on the floor. We helped His Majesty into the bath.

"So . . . Catherine," said the King, filling the water with putrid bubbles. "Good move?"

Mr. Heneage looked at me, eyes full of trepidation, as if to communicate a wordless warning. But I am certain. This time, it is different. And sometimes, to win in this life, you just have to put all your eggs in one basket.

"Divorced, beheaded, died," I said, pushing two stems of lavender up my nostrils. "Divorced, lived happily ever after."

## THE FACTS

It may sound like the worst job in the world, but most Tudors would've given their right arm to sit beside King Henry VIII while he strained away on his "close stool," a portable velvet-lined box containing the regal chamber pot. There, matters of national and often international importance would be discussed and mulled over, so being in the room offered enormous influence, if you were brave enough to chime in.

Beyond toilet duties, the groom dressed the King, oversaw his household finances and the signing of documents, while mediating with nosy government ministers and wives who wanted to know all the latest gossip.

After his third wife, Jane Seymour, died in 1537, Henry remained single and miserable for two years, before his chief minister, Thomas Cromwell, had an idea. Keen to make allies abroad, Cromwell looked to the European continent for a suitable spouse and eventually zoned in on the 24-year-old Düsseldorf-born Anne, daughter of the mainly Protestant Duke of Cleves. Cromwell commissioned Hans Holbein the Younger to paint a portrait of Anne and the King liked what he saw, only then to be disappointed when he met her in real life. The King's revulsion is well documented, cementing Anne's reputation as Henry's "ugly Queen."

This was particularly unfair given the state of the man himself. His athletic days behind him, the bloated 49-year-old had already started deteriorating physically and certainly wasn't setting any hearts aflutter. He suffered from bouts of melancholy and rage, along with gout, syphilis and chronic constipation, meaning he spent a great deal of time in his private chambers.

Suffice to say there wasn't much of a spark between Henry and Anne, and their marriage was annulled after just six months. For Anne, of course, this was a stroke of luck as it meant she wouldn't be impregnated—a dangerous predicament in Tudor times—or have her head chopped off like poor Anne Boleyn. Instead, as is now known, Anne of Cleves became the second "divorced" queen in the rhyme,* the King awarding her the honorary title of the King's Sister, £500 a year, and two palaces, where she lived happily (unmarried) ever after.

Thomas Cromwell wasn't quite so lucky. Word of the King's inability to consummate his marriage spread rapidly around the English court, and Cromwell was accused of being a little tattletale. His rivals in the Royal Household sought to capitalize on the King's humiliation, and after being charged with more unforgivable wrongdoings, Cromwell was arrested and taken to the Tower of London, where he was condemned to death without trial. On 28 July, the same day Henry married Catherine Howard, Cromwell was executed on Tower Hill, a decision Henry would later regret.

As for the grooms, unlike Henry Norris who lost his head for throwing his lot in with wife number two (Cromwell played a big part in doing him in), Thomas Heneage managed to keep his position until his retirement in 1546. No doubt thrilled, Denny finally got the top job and all the esteem and leverage it offered, only for the King to keel over and die a year later.

*The popular rhyme relating to King Henry VIII's six wives goes as follows: "Divorced (Catherine of Aragon), beheaded (Anne Boleyn), died (Jane Seymour), divorced (Anne of Cleves), beheaded (Catherine Howard), survived (Catherine Parr)."

While short-lived, Denny's tenure certainly wasn't unproductive. His years of faithful service made him one of Henry's closest confidants, raising his rank among other members of the court. Because of this, he was able to help the dying monarch finalize his will and heavily influence arrangements for the succession, making him, for a short spell at least, one of the most powerful men in England.

Mayhaps, just mayhaps, the smell was worth it after all.

# 7.

## *The Royal Oak*

In 1649, after years of civil war between Royalists, who supported the monarchy, and Parliamentarians (or "Roundheads"), who wanted to abolish it, King Charles I of England, Scotland and Ireland was finally defeated and sent to the scaffold to have his head chopped off. With no one on the throne, England briefly became a republic known as the "Commonwealth," headed up by Thomas Cromwell's great-great-grand-nephew, Oliver.

King Charles's son, also called Charles (there were only so many names to go around), vowed to avenge his father, reverse the revolution and restore the monarchy. After being anointed King of Scotland, he went to war with Cromwell and his Parliamentarians in an effort to retake the throne of England too. But in 1651, the 21-year-old lost a decisive battle and was forced to flee, taking refuge in Boscobel Woods in Shropshire.

The story of young Charles's daring escape has become the stuff of legend, the intricate details dying with the few people involved. But in 2015, when microbiologists placed electrodes in the soil of Boscobel to learn more about the ancient wood, instead of the numerical data they had been expecting, they got prose—lots and lots of it. The forest had a story to tell them, it said, and they'd be wise to get comfortable. The microbiologists pressed "record," lay down in the grass, and received the tale of a forest, a tree and a runaway king, all with remarkably good grammar.

---

We are the ancient cycle, the breathing, photosynthesizing whole, where life comes and goes but never ends. We are the flourishing and the decaying, the towering and the tiny, the symphony and the silence. Or Boscobel Woods, for short.

Beneath the soil, we remember it all. Our Wood Wide Web, the underground fungal network that connects every tree and shrub, holds in its twisting, complex threads tales of Viking invasions and lovers' feuds, of tribal hunts and the woodpeckers being particularly aggressive that one year. But it is under the rotten stump of the Royal Oak where the mycorrhizal memories glow the brightest.

"For the last time, I'm not the King!" barked the Oak to a fledgling young sapling in the late spring many years ago. He'd just bequeathed her a quart of phosphorus, to help strengthen her roots and, thinking it was proper, the sapling responded with a "You humble me, your great and noble highness, I am not worthy."

The Oak was a dyed-in-the-bark Republican, so, understandably, talk of kings made him uncomfortable. But his status in the forest was hard to deny.* Standing mighty among his

---

*The English oak tree (*Quercus robur*) has long held a special place in the culture and hearts of the English. They are often the biggest, most beautiful trees in the landscape, their wide-spreading boughs and acorns supporting a diverse range of wildlife. The majestic, sacred significance of the oak

neighbors with his broad trunk, sprawling limbs and thick body of leaves, it was almost impossible not to look up to him. Oaks before him had always been the Kings of the Forest, not only for their stature, but also because they supported more life than any other species in England and perhaps, even, the world.

"Stop that!" the Oak would say to the beetles and squirrels who thanked him for his protection, or to the mosses and lichens who knelt at his feet. "I'm not the King! There should be no kings!"

Except for a small group of hedgehogs who were trying to revive the direct democracy model of Ancient Athens, in Boscobel, the Oak was alone in his political views. So when a revolution stirred among the humans, with republicans promising to topple the Crown and implement parliamentary democracy, he became obsessed.

Out in Shropshire, we had always relied on animals to bring us news from the outside world. While the completion of Hadrian's Wall and the end of Henry VIII's fifth marriage had very little bearing on us, we'd listen with mild curiosity to the daily reports from London and beyond. It was always the birds who broke stories first, bringing with them accounts of recent battles and fresh scandals within hours. From time to time we got a tidbit from a relay system of well-meaning snails, but the news was always centuries old before it reached us.

"Rome's fallen," they told us in 1924.

The Oak lived for these dispatches, religiously devouring every update on the groundbreaking campaign to free the En-

---

extends across Europe and history, with ancient rulers wearing crowns of oak leaves, illustrative of the tree's long association with gods and kings.

glish from their unelected overlord. He learned everything there was to know about Oliver Cromwell, the man leading the charge against King Charles I, and became so fanatical he got a woodpecker to carve "Crazy for Crommers" into his trunk.*

Over the years, we patiently listened to his lectures and rants whenever he chose to have one, following every fight and maneuver in the civil war, until King Charles I was defeated, captured and beheaded. An intrinsic supporter and protector of life, the execution itself did not sit well with the Oak, but he was soon able to rationalize it. "Well, it's not the way I would've done it," he said. "But I'm sure they know what they're doing."

As King Charles I's son wrestled to take back his birthright, we started to get a bit sick of hearing so much about an affair that would never affect us.

"It affects us all!" the Oak would say. None of us believed him, of course, until it did.

We first felt his footsteps in the early hours of 4 September 1651, when he arrived at the White Ladies Estate on the fringes of the woods. Miles away, the ground had shaken under the Battle of Worcester where Charles II had made a last-ditch attempt to crush Cromwell and take back control. Three thousand of his men had died, and he had no choice but to run.†

---

*After decades of building tension between the Crown and Parliament, the English Civil War kicked off in earnest in 1642. Nine long years of conflict later, the Parliamentarians finally defeated those loyal to the monarch, and the country became a republic. The military commander Oliver Cromwell would become Lord Protector of England, Scotland and Ireland from 1653.
†The Battle of Worcester took place on 3 September 1651 and saw Cromwell's New Model Army overpower Charles II's largely Scottish Royalist force, marking the final fight of the war. The Royalists were dubbed "Cava-

He jumped off his horse in heavy, rain-soaked boots and tried to make out the houses and barns in the darkness.

"So this is the castle that's to shelter a king?" said the precocious young man to the men who had escorted him. He looked across at the ruins of an old priory, crumbling beside the main house, receding into the gloom. "Are you sure about this, Giffard?"

Major Giffard, whose cousins owned the estate, side-eyed the rider next to him.

"These are good people, sire. They'll keep you safe, while we consider our next move."

Within minutes, the woods were alive with the red-hot gossip. Every Ash, Birch and Beech was starstruck.

"I beg your pardon?!" said the Oak on hearing the news.

"Oh my God, a royal visit!" said a nearby Cedar.

"All hail the King!" said the Royalist Birch who grew beside the Oak.

"He's not the King! He's an enemy of the state!" yelled the Oak.

"AHHHHHHHHHHHHH!" screamed an overexcited sapling.

Major Giffard, flanked by Royalist soldiers, approached the main house and rapped loudly on its front door.

"Who goes there?" came a high, muffled voice.

"We're here to see the Giffards," replied the major.

"They're not 'bout, I'm afraid. Might I take a message?" asked the man.

---

liers" from the Latin word meaning horsemen. Meanwhile, the Parliamentarians' bad haircuts were immortalized in history with the less glamorous name of "Roundheads."

"Who am I speaking to?"

"George Penderell, sir."

"Are your parents in, George?"

"I'm 37."

"Oh."

"I looks after the place while the Giffards are away."

"Excellent. Then I think you might be able to help us."

"You'd leave my fate in the hands of a *housekeeper*?" scoffed Charles under his breath, ready to turn away.

"Are you a Royalist, Mr. Penderell?" asked the major.

"Ummmm . . . that depends, dunnit, on whether ye are?"

The major smiled. "Would you be so kind as to open the door?" he said.

"How do I know ye're not one of them Roundheads?" asked George.

"I can assure you, we're quite the opposite," said the major.

"Promise?"

"Promise."

George opened the door and squinted at the haggard faces through the orange glow of his lantern.

"Mr. Penderell, I wonder if you might put up an old friend of mine, just for the night," said the major.

"Right . . . " said George, rubbing his eyes. "Who is it?"

The major stepped aside, and in an opening between the huddled bodies, Charles spun around and presented himself like a prize. George's sleepy eyes grew wide and before anyone knew it, his lantern had smashed on the floor and plunged them all into darkness.

While frustrated with the quality of his new lodgings and the stature of his hosts, Charles ordered his Royalist comrades to disband, leaving only him and one other ally, Lord Wilmot, at the White Ladies Estate. Roundhead troops were surely sweeping the area, and the King wanted to be invisible. Or at least that is what a vine growing through a crack in the bricks told us.

As the Royalists peeled off into the night, George Penderell's more resourceful brother, Richard, was sent for, most likely because he was much better at this sort of thing, and he soon arrived at the house. Inside, the men's silhouettes moved about in the flicker of candles and lanterns, busy plotting until the pink wash of sunrise heralded a new day.

The Oak was pleased when a chaffinch told us Charles's companions had barely made it a few miles before being captured by Roundheads, but less pleased to discover that the King got the tip-off too.

Richard Penderell, sleepy and disheveled, emerged from the house in a hurry and gave the all-clear to the King, who stepped out in disguise. Sporting a deeply unfortunate new haircut, stained clothing and a greasy old hat, Charles looked more like a peasant than the heir to the throne. He moved uneasily in his rough, linen shirt and itchy trousers, with the disgruntled expression of a tree that only went in for a trim, but came out a stump.*

"What's he supposed to be, then?" asked a Hawthorn, watching from the edge of the property.

---

*The King's foray into the art of disguise is well documented. According to one contemporary account, "His Majesty had been advised to rub his hands on the back of the chimney, and with them his face, in order to a disguise, and some person had cut off his locks of hair: His Majesty, having put off his blue riband, buff-coat, and other princely ornaments, put on a noggen course [sic] shirt . . . green suit, and leather doublet." Another account has it that walnut leaves were used to dye the King's pale skin.

"Poor," said another.

George, still nervous, waved goodbye from the front door as the scruffy King followed Richard into the trees, reaching to scratch itches that crawled up his back and hobbling in shoes much too small for him.

"He'll get blisters," said a worried old Elm.

But blisters were the least of his worries. The heavy gray clouds that had been holding on all night finally let go. Richard and Charles trudged on with their coats over their heads, but got soaked to the bone nonetheless.

"I can git ye as far as Wolverhampton, sire," said Richard as they walked, speaking loudly over the downpour.

"You will take me as far as I require!"

Charles had divulged his plan to part ways with his close companion, Lord Wilmot, and reunite in London, where he hoped his supporters would help him gain passage to France.

"Beg pardon, sire, but the way's fraught with peril. If we're caught, 'twill be the end o' me."

"I can't think of a higher honor for a man of your station."

"Are you hearing this?" bellowed the Oak as the conversation trickled through our lines.

"He means it in a nice way," said the Birch.

"Okay . . . " said Richard. "It's just, the path t'ward London's gonna be swarmin' with Roundheads, and I reckon it'd be—"

"You're forgetting, Mr. . . . ?"

"Penderell, sire."

"Penderell. It has been ordained, by divine right, that I shall wear the crown, and rule these kingdoms. Do you think a few Roundhead traitors can usurp God's—"

"ANYTHING?" came a man's voice from afar, bouncing off

trunks and branches, disguising its origins. Richard fell flat on the ground, pushing Charles down with him. They sank into the wet mud beneath them.

"Nah," came another. Charles watched through the tangle of trees as two Roundhead soldiers met, chatted and then jumped on their horses and rode away. He remained on the ground until he was sure they were gone and waited a bit longer to be safe.

"That were close," said Richard.

Charles jumped up and wiped the mud off his face, equal parts furious and grateful. Richard, not quite as agile as the young king, held out a hand for a lift, but Charles was busy brushing down his trousers.

"If not London," said the King through gritted teeth, "then where?"

Richard struggled to his feet alone.

"I mean, if I had my say, Yer Majesty," he said, "I'd head for Wales."

A new plan was drawn up. With a strong faction of Royalist supporters in Wales, and a quicker route to the coast, the King decided to follow Richard's advice and travel west. They resolved to stay hidden until nightfall when they would set off along the road. In the meantime, Richard decided the King's peasant persona needed some finessing.

"So what do you think of Oliver Cromwell?" asked Richard.

"Oh, this is ridiculous," said Charles.

"Play along, sire. We could be questioned at any time!"

"He's great," said Charles, rolling his eyes.

"Why d'you think that then?"

"Because I'm an idiot peasant."

"Sire?"

"Because he's taking back control."

"Good, good," said Richard. "And why don't you like the King?"

"Because I don't believe in rulers. I think we'd be better off directionless and untethered, like a ship without a captain."

"Okay, maybe let's just work on the accent instead," said Richard. "Repeat after me: fair morn to ye, just off t' fields fer work."

"Why would I have to . . . ?"

"Just say it."

Charles closed his eyes and swallowed the indignity.

"Fair morning to you, just off to the fields for work," he said slowly.

"Fair *morn* to *ye*, just off t' fields *fer* work."

"Fair morning to ye. Just off tee-fields, for work."

"Fair *morn* to ye."

"Fair morn to ye."

"Just off t' fields fer work."

"Just off tee the fields fir work."

"We'll just say ye're a mute," said Richard, giving up and moving on to address what he referred to as Charles's "royal walk."

"Yer chin's still too high," he barked, evaluating the King as he walked back and forth in front of him. "Do it like ye're bowing!"

"I don't bow! I'm the King!" snapped Charles. Nearby, a patch of mushrooms tutted.

"Well, loosen yer knees then!" said Richard.

"Loosen your knees then, *Your Majesty!*" said Charles, growing increasingly frustrated. Richard held out his palms in apology.

Charles tucked his chin, bent his knees and ambled up and down, looking predictably ridiculous. Richard couldn't hold back his laughter and received a killer glare, undermined somewhat by the faintest of smiles.

"We're done here," said the King, remembering himself. "It should be you peasants changing your walks, not me. Honestly, it's a wonder you get anywhere at all, moving like that."

They left as soon as darkness fell and reached the road shortly after. The last time we felt their footsteps was just before 8 pm, when a Horse-Chestnut sapling reported she had just been squashed.

"Good riddance," boomed the Oak through the lines that night. "With any luck they'll be arrested by sunrise and this whole farce can be put to bed for once and for all."

But late the next night, the downtrodden sapling sent another message. "HE'S BACK! xxx" it read. The network lit up again as excited plants speculated themselves silly.

A jackdaw informed us later that Charles and Richard had arrived at the home of a trusted ally in Madeley, a town on the way to Wales, and learned that the River Severn, separating England from their destination, was heavily guarded by Roundheads. His plans dashed, Charles made the decision to return to Boscobel and reassess.

He arrived at Boscobel House, another building nestled deep in our interior, in the dead of night. Managed by another of the five Penderell brothers, Boscobel House was more remote than the White Ladies Estate, being cradled by trees on all sides, and as such had been the hiding spot of choice for many a priest and persecuted Catholic throughout the years.

A Beech whose branches draped over the windows watched as Charles and Richard stumbled inside, exhausted, starving and soaking wet. Charles collapsed into a chair as Richard's brother William, the caretaker of the house, and his wife Joan rushed about to look after him. They pulled off his shoes and nursed his burning feet, cleaning the cuts and sores inflicted by the ill-fitting footwear. They hung his clothes by the fire and brought him back to life with bread, cheese and a splash of beer.*

Richard, not afforded such special attention, peeled off his own clothes, downed a cup of milk and collapsed half-naked in a corner.

"You shouldn't be in here, sire," came a voice as the sun crept through the open windows a few hours later.

The King, who had only just shut his eyes, opened them again, squinting through the sunlight to identify his mystery visitor.

"It's Careless!" said the man.

"I'm aware it's a risk, but I haven't slept in—"

"No, it's Careless. Colonel William Careless," said Colonel William Careless, an officer from Charles's army, stepping out from the shadows.†

---

*Other accounts verify the tender care given to the King, including that of his contemporary Thomas Blount: "The Col [William Careless] pull'd off his Majesties shoos, which were full of graven, and stockens which were very wet . . . the good wife put some hot embers in those to dry them, whilst his Majesties feet were washing and his stockens shifted . . . "

†William Careless, born to a Catholic family in Staffordshire, fought on the side of the Royalists in the civil war and alongside Charles at the Battle of Worcester, reputedly witnessing the last man to be slain in the battle.

"Careless!" said Charles. "When did you get here?"

"Yesterday evening, sire," said Careless.

"Are there others?" asked Charles. Careless shook his head.

"Just us, sire. But there's Roundheads everywhere. They've raided White Ladies and I reckon it's only a matter of time before they find this place. I've been in the priest hole all night but it's dangerous.* If they search the house there's a good chance they'll find it," said Careless.

"We head south then, to London," said Charles, getting up.

"Not yet, sire. We need to lie low somewhere. Let the Roundheads do a full sweep of the area so they rule it out, and then we can make a run for it."

"There's a grand old oak not far from the house," said Joan Penderell, coming in with some breakfast. "Ye could hide half an army up there." Charles and Careless wolfed down their meals—some suspicious-looking mushrooms Joan had picked that morning from the usual place—and followed her outside, leaving Richard still snoring away in the corner.

When word reached the Oak, he was fuming. "Over my dead stump!" he said. Though of course, he could do nothing but watch as Charles and Careless climbed inside, weaved through his branches and settled into a perfect cradle in the middle.

---

*Excelling at hide-and-seek was an essential skill for Catholic priests, depending on which king or queen had just inherited the throne. Like many great houses owned by Catholic families, Boscobel had priest holes built into walls and under floorboards, where priests could hide in the event of a search. Many were built during the time of Elizabeth I when Catholic religious services were outlawed. Boscobel House, which still stands today, has two priest holes, one under a closet (privy) and another under the stairs leading to the attic.

"Makes sense, you know," said Charles as he got comfortable.

"What does, sire?" asked Careless.

"An Oak tree. King of the Forest," said Charles, patting the branch next to him.

Careless laughed, thinking that was what Charles wanted, but soon realized it wasn't. "No, yeah, that's . . . , I didn't think about that, actually."

"No other tree comes close," said Charles, looking up at the sprawling canopy. "I mean, look at it."

Careless looked.

"Superior in every way," said Charles.

Careless wedged himself between two branches so the King could recline in the Oak's cradle and rest his head in his lap. "You should get some rest, Your Majesty. I'll watch you," he said. And so, the King, more comfortable than he had been in days, did just that.

Our lines were alive with activity. Every tree, weed and shrub was talking about the Oak and his unwelcome guest.

"So unfair! I want the King to climb on *me!*" said the Birch.

"Here, Oak, isn't that treason?" teased an old Ash.

The Oak tensed and squeezed, hoping to send the King tumbling, but his branches didn't so much as twitch. He was harboring a fugitive, whether he liked it or not.

"Are you a Royalist now, Oak?" asked the Beech.

"Never!" said the Oak. "I've always said—haven't I always said that the monarchy is an outdated and unjust system of hereditary privilege and absolute power that must be obliterated once and for all?! The sooner this twerp is captured and his fight for the throne is put to bed, England can enjoy true democracy. We can live in a republic that upholds the principles of liberty, accountability and the rule of law, ensuring that power belongs to all and not to a snotty little unelected brat! And what's more . . . "

The King stirred in Careless's lap and opened his eyes, for what seemed like the very first time. Immediately he noticed the leaves shivering above his head, each one meticulously crafted, greener than he had ever realized. He watched, for a moment, the thin fingers of the branch, with their nodules and bumps and buds, bobbing up and down in the breeze, and his hungry pupils agreed they were all that mattered, those twisted twigs and their dance.

". . . It's leaders we need! Not rulers! Rulers are in it for themselves, leaders are in it for the greater good!" continued the Oak.

Fingertips pressed to the ridges of the bark, Charles pushed himself up and wondered who had engineered the cradle he sat in, with its curving branches and quilt of green. He felt the line of the bough beneath his back and thighs, and marveled at how they could have known his shape.

His head fell back to find jays hopping on the arms above, while beneath them, crawling upside-down, a beetle, dwarfed by everything around it, traversed the mountains and valleys in the bark. Along it went, on its great odyssey, toward the trunk, where a woodpecker spun in circles, searching for a morsel over the forests of moss that bled from cracks and scars in the surface.

"It is not my *right* to be an Oak. It is my *duty!*"

Slowly, so as not to wake the sleeping Careless, Charles came to his feet and met the eyes of a squirrel who was collecting acorns on a neighboring branch. With its hands and mouth full, it scurried in the direction of the trunk and hopped out of sight. He went after it, arriving in the middle and swinging across to the other side, where a long bough reached down toward an opening. From there, peering out at the moss-carpeted earth below, he followed the trunk as it slipped beneath the soil and reached invisibly into the surrounding forest, where saplings sheltered from the elements and beeches and birches twirled into the sky.

"You may look up at me . . . "

Charles looked up at the towering world in front of him, and could see at once every level and layer, all teeming with insects and fungi and lichens. There was the whole universe, right there, busy with independent dependents, supported and protected by the King of the Forest who asked nothing in return, but got everything he needed.

". . . but I won't look down on you."

Charles's eyes grew wide with the intensity of someone who finally understood, and for a moment, he forgot himself entirely. By the time he realized he was losing his balance, it was already too late. Shoes scraping the bark, he tumbled backward, arms flailing, and crashed into the bough below with a yelp. He bounced off, and continued his undignified descent, managing, at the last moment, to wrap his hands around another branch. He hoisted himself up and hugged it, sobering up just in time to hear the troop of Roundhead soldiers fast approaching.

"Oak! Do something!" pleaded the Birch. The King was now fully exposed, lying there winded and frozen like a stunned pheasant.

"They're going to kill him!" added the Cedar.

"No they're not," said the Oak, pleased the ordeal would soon be over.

"Remember, Cromwell wants him alive . . . " came the gruff voice of one of the Roundheads from afar.

"See! He'll get a fair trial," said the Oak.

". . . so he can kill him in London," finished the Roundhead.

Their heavy footsteps got closer and closer as the Oak wrestled with an impossible dilemma. The King was trembling, and the Oak felt it in his rings. Support and protect had been his mantra, and the mantra of every Oak before him. Like a baby owl hiding from a hawk in his thick foliage, the shivering human clinging to his branch now begged silently for refuge.

With a furious grunt, the Oak started photosynthesizing on overdrive, straining and squeezing at the leafy limbs below the King, pulling them together, inch by inch.

The Birch and the Beech cheered him on, and the saplings screamed with delight. He pushed and pushed and pushed until the young shoots finally met and closed, enveloping Charles in a cloak of green.

"Lads, I've found the King!" shouted one of the Roundheads below. Charles winced as the others came running, their footsteps quick and heavy.

"Where?" shouted one of them, arriving out of breath and flustered. The rest trampled over.

The first Roundhead pointed up at the Oak. Charles held his breath.

"King of the Forest," he said, smiling. The others stared at him, incredulous.

"You prat!" barked the leader of the group.

"It's just a joke."

"I nearly fell in a ditch!"

"Well, sorry for trying to lighten the mood . . . "

The leader pulled down his stockings and urinated against the trunk.

"This is what I think of your King of the Forest," he said, sighing with relief.

"Oi mate, I wouldn't do that if I was you," said a different soldier.

"You what?" said the urinator.

"Nah, I'm just saying like, I'm a bit superstitious about this sort of stuff, and—"

"Are you lot hearing yourselves? You're meant to be advocates for parliamentary democracy and now you want me to curtsey in front of a big shrub you reckon has divine right to rule over the squirrels? King of the Forest?! Have you forgotten the whole point of what we've been doing these last five years? I mean, being anti-king is sort of the central facet of our whole thing! Honestly, you lot, I don't understand you sometimes," he said, putting himself away.

The soldiers trailed off toward the house and, forcing their way in, searched every wardrobe, cabinet and priest hole.

Charles hurried back to Careless, who had missed the whole episode conversing with a family of woodlice.

"There's something up with this tree, sire," said Careless, looking at his hands like they were worms.

"I am an acorn, Careless," said Charles.

"Well, I'm glad it's not just me," said Careless, clutching his forehead.

"And I'm going to be an oak."

"I beg your pardon, sire?"

"This," said Charles, gesturing up to the winding branches, "this is a king."

The Roundheads wrapped up their search of Boscobel

House and did one last sweep of the White Ladies Estate before finally giving up.

"He's long gone," said one of them as they jumped on their horses and rode away.

The Oak breathed a sigh of relief as Charles and Careless climbed down and returned to the house.

"Harboring an enemy of the state. That's punishable by death," said the Oak, devastated to have betrayed his beloved Republic. "I should just fell myself right now."

Back at the house, Joan Penderell prepared a chicken dinner for her grateful guests. Charles and Careless, checking there were no mushrooms, devoured it within minutes and licked their plates clean.

They stayed in the house that night, each sleeping on a pallet in one of the secret priest holes. The King was in the attic, cocooned by thick wooden boards. Another tree keeping him safe, this time from beyond the grave.

The Oak began his hours-long lamentation, begging for a great gust of wind to blow him over. The mycorrhizal threads beneath him did us all a favor and disconnected him until the morning.

According to a daddy longlegs who was holidaying in the house, Charles got up early and spent some time in prayer. Afterward he came down and made everyone brunch. Careless and the Penderells watched in disbelief as he danced around the kitchen preparing fried mutton collops by himself, refusing all offers of assistance.

"It's the least I could do," he said, serving Richard the biggest piece.

In the afternoon he came outside again, and back into our domain. He sat alone at a stone table under a shelter of vines and branches and looked to be deep in his thoughts. The vines listened as he narrated the plan forming in his head.

"Head to Moseley . . . new disguise . . . move down to Oxford . . . Or maybe Bristol? Bristol. And from there to the coast . . . Sorry, can I just—like, those mutton collops were really good. It's just I really nailed that. Like not even—"

"Sire," interrupted Careless, coming outside to fetch him. "It's time to get going."

It was decided all five Penderell brothers would escort the King to his next hideout in Moseley, a town to the south.

"The important thing is to keep moving," said Careless, bidding farewell. Charles embraced him and thanked him for his service.

"Be safe," said Charles.

"I will, sire," said Careless.

"And don't be careless."

"That might be difficult, sire."

As the Penderells prepared to leave, Charles quietly slipped off into the trees and made his way to the base of the Oak. He stood for some time in silence, listening to the jays up above, the squirrels scurrying along the branches and the leaves whistling in the wind. And then, checking that no one was watching, he took a step back and bowed.

We last felt his footsteps on the southern edge of the forest, walking with the five Penderell brothers by his side. A wren told us she saw him set off from Moseley a few days later, and a pigeon said he made it to Bristol. A badger claimed to have eaten him after a one-on-one death match, but that story was quickly disproved. All reports suggested the King was cheerful and courageous throughout his journey, and while he was recognized multiple times, he was never given away. Even with a high bounty on his head, it seemed the average Englishman was gunning for him and helping him on his way.*

After a grueling six weeks traveling under cover of night, dodging Roundheads and hiding in holes and cupboards, the King finally made it to the coast. There, some seagulls told us, he was smuggled onto a boat and across the channel to France.

"Well, I'm glad he's out of the picture," said the Oak. "Now Cromwell can focus on turning this country around."

Over the next ten years, Oliver Cromwell did just that, but not necessarily for the better. The changes he had been flirting with since the execution of Charles I were implemented in full force. And it wasn't the democratic revolution the Oak thought it might be.

Cromwell dissolved Parliament and made himself Lord Protector, giving himself permission to rule unelected over England.

"Sounds a lot like being a king . . . " said the Beech when we heard.

A family of crows kept us in the loop as the Lord Protector's Puritan regime swept across the country, picking away at all the things that made life worth living. Frivolous enjoyment and material pleasures were the enemy. Inns and taverns closed their doors. Theatres, playhouses and arenas were boarded up. Most sports were banned. If boys were caught playing football on Sundays, they'd be whipped.

---

*The reward for anyone passing information leading to Charles's capture was a colossal £1,000—something like a quarter of a million pounds in today's money. Anyone found helping to conceal Charles, meanwhile, would be given the equally enticing reward of "death without mercy."

Men and women were made to throw all color out of their wardrobes. Only black and modest clothes were permitted, in humble reverence to God. People could pollinate, but only if they promised not to have a nice time. Kissing, cuddling and dancing were the devil's delights and they had no place in a cleaned-up country.

When the first winter came, a tearful robin told us, "You can't say 'Christmas' anymore." Feasts were outlawed, with soldiers patrolling the streets in search of stuffing to confiscate. There were no more decorations, no more games, no more carol-singing and no more old ladies drunk on sherry. If you so much as thought about having fun on 25 December, you could find yourself in the stocks. Boscobel's holly bushes wept for weeks.

A stillness came over the forest. Children stopped climbing in the trees and young lovers no longer wrapped themselves in each other's arms beneath the Oak, lest they be seen. On May Day, no one tied ribbons to the branches of the Ash and danced around its trunk. There were no more parties thrown under the bough of the Beech beside Boscobel House and no more music played beneath the Cedar that loomed over the White Ladies Estate.

"I didn't vote for this!" cried the Oak. "This is not how it was supposed to be!"

The electricity which once buzzed beneath the forest floor fizzled away. Our lines dried out as every tree and plant fell into a stupor. Even the nettles, who hate the world and everything in it, couldn't escape the suffocating malaise.

"Admit it," croaked the Birch to the Oak one day in January. "You were wrong." The Oak, bare and stiff in the numbness of winter, said nothing.

The seasons came and went, all merging into one. Even spring struggled to stir life back into us. Birds stopped bringing news from the outside world, and before long we could barely remember the singing, the dancing and the kissing.

And then, one evening in the early summer of 1660, one of our lines crackled back to life. A message from the Ash. "RIB-BONS" it read.

The Beech lit up. "Long table. Colors! Many people!"

We felt the weight of their feet pressing down on us, gathering. Tiny footsteps ran rings around Boscobel House.

"I just got stepped on!" shrieked a buttercup. "INCREDI-BLE."

The Oak awoke from a depressed slumber to feel fingers wrapped around his branches, swinging and leaping.

"What's happening?" he said. Suddenly there was singing and dancing, a hundred feet bouncing and spinning over our mycorrhizal threads. The Oak's leaves brightened as life flushed back into them.

A relay-snail arrived to break the news, huffing and puffing. "Boudica's dead," it wheezed.

Fortunately, a passing blackbird was able to tell us something a little more up to date. Oliver Cromwell had died and, in a suspiciously king-like move, had named his son Richard as successor. Richard, however, was not up to the job and after barely a year, the whole thing fell apart.

As a power vacuum widened, Parliament wondered whether they should just go back to having a king again, and after a short deliberation, the throne was taken out of storage and given a quick polish.

A new king was anointed, and he immediately set about repealing Cromwell's strict Puritan laws. He opened the inns and theatres, loosened religious restrictions and let the kids dance again. Everyone dusted off their red hats and sparkly shoes and lived in full color once more.

"Who is it?" asked the Oak, secretly hoping for one name in particular. "What's he called?"

"King Charles II," said the blackbird. "But they call him the Merry Monarch."

The forest sang with the news. The young man we sheltered a decade ago had returned and breathed new life into the country. He ruled alongside Parliament, willingly reducing the authority of his office to give power back to the people.*

"Well, it's not perfect," said the Oak, "but I suppose it's a step in the right direction."

Later that summer we felt the familiar rhythm of his footsteps. Flanked by aides and guards, King Charles II hopped off his carriage at Boscobel House and was welcomed by his old friends the Penderells. He hugged and kissed each of them, reaffirming his eternal gratitude, and went inside to eat the special lunch he had requested.

After licking his plate clean, the King stood down his entourage and walked into the woods alone, retracing the hurried steps he'd taken ten years before. He arrived at the Oak and looked up at the great boughs twisting into the green.

He bowed, grabbed hold of a low-hanging branch and disappeared into the blanket of leaves.

"What's happening?" asked the Birch. "Tell us!"

---

*Though previous English monarchs had given up some of their divine rights (perhaps most notably, King John when he signed the Magna Carta in 1215), this was usually a desperate attempt to avoid war or regicide. Charles's concessions—though limited—were unprecedented.

But the Oak didn't say anything.

The King climbed up into the cradle and folded himself inside, remembering how it had been engineered just for him.

"The Crown owes you a great debt," he said, reaching up and touching the branch above his head. "And your country too." His hand brushed over gouges in the surface, deep depressions he hadn't noticed before. He craned his neck and saw "Crazy for—" carved in the bark, the rest obscured by moss. He stretched to scrape it clean but was distracted when five acorns fell, perfectly synchronized, onto his head.

"Listen," said the Oak. The King looked up and out across the twirling branches. "If there *has* to be a king, then I'm glad it is you."

The King chuckled and readjusted himself in the cradle, so that its curve met the line of his back.

"I knew you'd come round eventually," he said, sinking into the bough and letting the whole world spin.

## THE FACTS

In 1651, England had been without a monarch for two and a half years. The King had been executed and his son and heir Charles was on the run, having been crushed by Oliver Cromwell's Parliamentarian army at Worcester. With the civil war over, Charles II urgently had to flee the country, or else suffer the same fate as his father. A large bounty on his head and a massive manhunt to find him meant he had to keep himself hidden and rely on the goodwill and loyalty of his English subjects. Having ridden 40 miles under the cover of darkness, Charles—recently crowned as King of Scotland—arrived at a north Shropshire estate owned by the Catholic Giffard family and looked after by the tenant farmers and servants, the Penderell brothers.

King Charles's daring escape is corroborated by many contemporary accounts, including one dictated by the King himself to the famous diarist Samuel Pepys, best known for his thrilling adventures in hiding cheese (and almost for his exclusive interview with the Plague). Putting themselves at considerable risk, the Penderells hid Charles at White Ladies Estate and gave him the opposite of a glow-up, hoping he might pass as a lowly peasant if questioned. Originally planning to escape to Wales, Charles was forced to head back to Boscobel where he and his fellow fugitive William Careless spent the day hidden in an oak tree. There, as the King himself recalled, they could "see soldiers going up and down in the thickest o' the wood searching for persons escaped . . . " After a night hiding in a priest hole, the King left Boscobel the following evening and was on the run for a further six weeks, evading capture by a hair's whisker, before secretly sailing on a coal brig to France and remaining abroad for the next nine years.

During Charles's exile, the country was governed as a republic, first under Parliament and then from 1653 under Oliver Cromwell as Lord Protector. Like the King before him, Cromwell argued with and even dismissed Parliament, although, unlike the King, he was able to exert control with a large standing army. Cromwell divided England into 11 areas, each governed by an army general, and began to radically reform the Church in line with Puritan values. This involved stripping churches of ornaments and abolishing *The Book of Common Prayer,* which in turn swept away many of the festivals and rituals that punctuated people's lives. Traditional activities such as May Day celebrations were banned, inns and playhouses were closed, feast days became fasting days and Christmas was officially cancelled. The only entertainment was the regular threat of execution for those who broke the rules.

Perhaps not unsurprisingly, many people found life a bit rubbish under the Protectorate and were only too glad to have a king back on the throne in 1660. Over the previous two years, Oliver Cromwell had suddenly died and his son Richard, a useless successor, had been forced to resign. Charles was invited back from exile to restore the monarchy, and everyone agreed to just pretend the last 11 years hadn't happened. On the day of his 30th birthday, 29 May 1660, Charles rode triumphantly back into London and set about resurrecting much of what had been suppressed under Cromwell. Feeling particularly festive, Charles had Cromwell's body exhumed and hung in chains, before placing his head on a spike above Westminster Hall where it somehow remained for 24 years.

The King never forgot his weeks on the run and would often commandeer conversations to retell the tale of his remarkable escape. His day spent hiding in the oak was always central to the story, so much so that the public holiday created—by act of Parliament—to commemorate the restoration of the Stuart monarchy was named "Royal Oak Day." May Day festivities and betrothals of marriages once again could resume under the boughs of the great oak, while beer lovers could swig back their ale in the hundreds of public houses rechristened "The Royal Oak," all in honor of the most majestic of trees.

By 1880, after two centuries' worth of careless tourists sawing off branches and tearing away chunks of bark as souvenirs, the Royal Oak died. It would live on, however, through a new tree propagated from the original, known as "the Son of the Royal Oak." Another century later, the Prince of Wales, later King Charles III, planted an acorn from the "Son" in the woods at Boscobel in memory of his ancestor. He might have to wait a while, though, before it's big enough to hide in.

# 8.

# *The Last Dodo*

In 1658, after 20 years plundering its natural resources and driving many of its native species to the brink of extinction, the Dutch East India Company* decided that building a colony on Mauritius, a small uninhabited island in the Indian Ocean, perhaps wasn't worth all the effort.

The failed settlers rounded up their Malagasy slaves and got back on their ships, pleased to say goodbye and good riddance to the tropical island that never wanted them. But when the final ship raised anchor and headed home, reports suggest not everyone made it onboard.

Until recently, the circumstances surrounding this curious footnote in history were frustratingly unclear, but when a memoir in a bottle washed up on Blackpool beach in 2020, the centuries-old story finally came to light.

*The Dutch ruled the seas in this period, establishing a global empire in Asia, the Americas and coastal areas of Africa. The Dutch East India Company (known as VOC in Dutch) made huge profits from a global trade in goods and slaves, a practice continued by other European colonizers. People were abducted from their native homes—including the island of Madagascar—transported on cramped ships and forced to work in inhumane, dangerous conditions.

Below is that memoir, scraped clean of barnacles and translated from Dutch.

––––––––––––

"Schnippel schnoppel kloppen slappen dippen doppen," or thereabouts, said Governor Abraham Evertszoon* when inspecting us the day we arrived. I later learned, after picking up his strange language, that he'd said something along the lines of "Help us transform this inhospitable island and perhaps we won't kill you." A storm was sweeping in from the sea and lashing our bare bodies with its torrents, stinging the VOC emblems that had just been branded onto our upper arms. We all nodded and got to work repairing the shelters that had blown down in the night, while the Governor ran inside and changed out of his wet clothes.

I was 15 when I was abducted by the pink men with funny accents and wooden shoes. They stole me and hundreds of others from our homes in Madagascar and transported us across the ocean to Mauritius, where we were put to work farming, building and chopping down trees.

The island fought back against those trying to master her, and while us Malagasy were well suited to her tropical tempers, the pink men struggled. She smothered them in thick, stifling heat, swarmed them with mosquitos and whipped up storms and cyclones to raze whatever they tried to build. Twenty years after their arrival, and one year after mine, the pink men finally held up their hands and surrendered.

We were being ferried to the last ship off the island when

––––––––––––

*Records verify that the Dutch official Governor Abraham Evertszoon ruled Mauritius from 1656 to 16 July 1658, when the island was abandoned.

one of the boys broke free and leaped into the water. It had crossed my mind too, and, in the confusion, I followed him in. Our master—a fat merchant we called Tomato Frog because of his forever sunburned face—screamed curses as we thrashed through the water. I could hear my Malagasy brothers cheering, until the loud bang of a gun struck them dumb.

"Good luck, Governor of Nothing!" yelled Tomato Frog as I kicked.

The gentle waves delivered me to the beach, exhausted. When I caught my breath, I realized I was alone. The other boy drifted lifelessly toward the shore, surrounded by a spill of red, while out in the blue, the great white sails and tiny pink heads melted into the horizon, and were gone.

I buried the boy, whose name I never knew, and went to live in the Governor's house, sleeping on his bed and wearing his discarded clothes. His shirts and jackets were much too big for me, but his hat fitted perfectly. I wore it everywhere, exploring my abandoned kingdom and salvaging what I could from the collapsed shelters and rotting storehouses. The rats, brought and left by the pink men, made quick work of the barrels of flour and grain, and the pigs sniffed out what was left, saving very little for me.

As I lay alone in my sunken bed listening to the creaking cabins strain against the elements, I wondered if the other boys had been taken to Amsterdam and freed. I imagined them clothed and smiling, clacking around in their wooden shoes, living in homes stacked high in the sky.

Mauritius worked day and night to undo her scars, and soon the gales razed what remained of the settlement. I packed up what I could and headed up the coast, leaving the pests to colonize the rubble.

·   ·   ·

All up the beaches I weaved between scattered crates and discarded logs, with every step another memento of the pink
men. Around the corner, Dutch pigs, with their frizzy blond
hairs, munched away at some dead bird's carcass. Dashed on
the rocks, bleached bones lay tangled in old fishing nets and
beside them, the great shells of giant tortoises sat hollow, the
wind whistling through them.* Inland I found the vast fields of
stumps where precious ebony trees once stood. Beside them,
the carts we'd used to carry the logs into ships bound for Holland lay splintered and sinking.

It seemed to me there wasn't a spot left unspoiled, until,
padding along the sand, I sighted a small island across the way.
Separated from the mainland by a 50-foot stretch of water and
protected from the rats, pigs and men who couldn't be bothered to wade across, the islet was a time capsule, a sanctuary—
it was Fialofana.† A thick forest of ebony trees sprang from the
middle, and around it, on the sandy beaches and craggy rocks,
giant tortoises still ambled. Birds filled the jungle canopy with
their songs and, down on the ground, ambling about without
a care in the world, were dodos, the stocky flightless birds long
since vanished from the mainland.

The peculiar-looking creatures, standing waist high with big
feet and even bigger beaks, were fearless. In fact, as I waded into

---

*Giant tortoises once criss-crossed Mauritius and its outlying islets. Ac-
counts tell of Dutch sailors riding on their large shells as well as slaughtering vast numbers for food and oil. Much like their human counterparts,
invasive European animals ravaged the local population, eating their eggs
and hatchlings, resulting in the extinction of the species by around 1700.
†*Fialofana* in Malagasy translates as sanctuary or shelter.

their pristine world, they assembled to welcome me. I don't expect they'd ever seen a man before, for they approached with the curiosity of a child, expecting no ill will. Even as I reached out to touch one, it didn't flinch, but instead came closer to investigate my hand. Their cousins on the mainland must have been easy meals, plodding blindly into hungry mouths.

Only one thing seemed to frighten them, and it was one of their own. She came hurtling out of the jungle, a ball of gray and white feathers, with one long leg and one short leg making her swing from side to side like a ship in a storm. Her inefficient but determined run scattered the welcoming committee and left me alone on the beach, awaiting her audience.

She arrived much too fast, losing control as she tried to slow down and falling flat on her face before me. She picked herself up, shook off the sand and took me in, tilting her head left and right.

"Hello," I said. She took a few steps back, to get a better view, and struggled to balance her lopsided body. I looked across at the other dodos who were watching from afar. "So, this is *your* island?"

She grunted and stared at me a little longer, before turning around and waddling toward the trees. When I didn't immediately follow, she looked back and squawked. I did what I was told and followed her.

After a slow, noisy journey in which she slipped and stumbled over almost every possible obstacle, we finally arrived at a shallow cave nestled deep in the trees. She bundled inside, yapping at me to join her, and had me sit on the ground. When I tried to get up, she yelled and yelled until I sat back down. So there I stayed, awaiting further instructions as she assembled twigs around me.

"Of course, Governess," I said, laughing, when she demonstrated where I should lay my head.

From that day on, wherever I went, she waddled on after me. Where I climbed, she stood at the bottom and squawked until I came down. Being alone was simply not an option. But I couldn't have chosen a better home if I'd tried. Perfectly situated in the center of the jungle, the thick wall of trees and curving roof of the cave gave ample protection from the elements. A freshwater stream ran alongside, enough to drink and wash in, and just a few minutes' walk along its banks was the shore.

Over the coming days I built upon the natural shelter, extending its footprint with a palm roof. I unpacked what I had taken from Old Grand Port—clothes, canvas, tools and gunpowder—and rolled out the Governor's mattress. I built a hearth for the fire and a spit on which to cook the fish. Sticks became spears and coconut shells became bowls.

The Governess observed the renovations with great interest and fiercely protected me as I worked. If a fly so much as looked at me the wrong way, she'd send it packing. If I climbed too high upon the rocks, she'd squawk madly until I came back down to safety.

Even in sleep, she wouldn't leave my side. Nestled in my arms against the warmth of my chest, she watched dutifully as the lapping waves and jungle chorus carried me off to sleep. And like this, weeks passed. Days exploring, building and fishing, nights cooking, sleeping and dreaming. For the briefest time, I wanted for nothing. I was the Governor of Everything, master of the island with my three-foot Governess. And then along came the boy.

.    .    .

I was knee deep in the water, hovering over a school of fish, ready to spear, when the Governess jumped up from her perch on the rocks, rolled onto the sand and bounded down the beach, screeching. It didn't take long to catch up.

The dodo welcoming committee had assembled by the crossing, crowding around something on the ground. When they heard the Governess speeding toward them, they quickly scattered, revealing a body lying face down in the sand.

I ran ahead, my breath stolen, and was certain he was dead. When I turned him over, his blond hair fell away to reveal a delicate face red with sunburn. He was about my age, I thought. A boy. The ocean gave no clues as to his origins. There was no sinking ship on the horizon or band of men desperately paddling to safety.

The Governess finally arrived and scrambled on top of him, nipping at his shredded undershirt and jumping on his chest. He jolted upright and coughed out a lungful of seawater, sending us both tumbling backward. He looked at me, eyes wild, and then, surrendering to the weight of his head, flopped lifeless onto the sand.

He woke up in the long shadow of a palm tree across the water, on the mainland. Despite the Governess's objections, I'd carried him on my back and dropped him there as the sun climbed down from the sky, setting everything ablaze. Hidden, I waited for him to sit up and find the parcel of fish and coconut shell filled with freshwater I'd left at his side. He looked around, confused, before devouring it all.

I returned home, certain the high tide would keep him away, and tried to reason with the Governess, who plodded alongside me in a strop.

"He's Dutch! Get a hold of yourself!" I told her. She honked back in contention.

"Yeah, well, you've never been to the mainland," I said. "Because of them, there's none of you left."

She clicked her beak.

"Maybe he'll get you too."

She clicked it some more.

"He's one of them. It doesn't matter if he looks nice," I said, but she just turned her head and pretended not to listen.

She didn't speak to me that night, and chose to sleep alone on the other side of the cave, committed to her grudge. The buzzes, chirps and warbles tried to take me away, but my mind was busy drawing the outline of his face and the shape of his body in the sand.

He was nowhere to be seen the next day, just as I had hoped, and the day after that, I was certain he was gone for good, off to try his own luck. The Governess soon forgot why she was angry at me, and the normal order of things resumed. We fished, explored and foraged. I swam in the sea and washed in the stream, made fires on the beach and watched the stars tear streaks in the sky. But every time I closed my eyes, I saw him dead, dashed on the rocks or floating face down in the shallows.

I don't know how many days passed before I decided to go and look for him, if only to catch a glimpse and put my mind at rest. The tide was high when I set out, so I had to swim. The Governess screeched as I kicked across to the mainland, furious at being left behind, but she eventually wore herself out and plopped down in the sand to wait for my return.

Hopping between jutting rocks and under arching palm trees that had been bent over the beach by endless storms, I rounded the first corner and felt my heart leap at the sight of him. He stood knee deep in the water with his drawers pulled up to his thighs, a giant water-lily pad tied to his head using the last shreds of his shirt as string. He hovered over a school of fish with a stick in his hands and, waiting for the opportune moment, threw it down and slapped the water. The fish scattered, thankful for the warning and left the boy to figure out what went wrong.

"I can show you," I said, coming up behind him. He swung round, blunt stick at the ready.

"Schnippel-slappen-kloppen-ploppen," he blurted, eyes wide. The panic dissolved immediately. "It's you! Klippity kloppety slip slop."

I asked him to slow down. Fast Dutch was still nonsense to me.

"I thought you were someone else," he said slowly, lowering his lethal weapon, half-delirious.

"Are there more?" I said, looking into the trees, stretching endlessly along the coastline. "From the shipwreck?" The boy squinted.

"Shipwreck?"

I tried to think of a different word.

"Your boat. Is it underwater?"

The boy frowned.

"I don't know. It left without me. It was the last one," he said. It must have been a month or two, who knows, since Tomato Frog and the pink men packed up and sailed away.

We stood and stared at each other as he caught his breath.

He was smaller than I had been picturing him, his face even more delicate, and, as his chest rose and fell, I thought he might topple over.

"I am Floris," he said, holding out his hand. I took it and wiggled it up and down, as I had seen the pink men do.

"I am the Governor," I said. Floris giggled and doffed his water-lily hat.

He had been living off rainwater and raw sea snails all this time, he told me, and hadn't slept in days.

"It was an accident," he said as I showed him how to sharpen a stick into a spear. "They told me to fetch some topsail polish from the storehouse on the island, just as we were leaving. I couldn't find it. By the time I got back to the dock, everyone was gone."

"You were on the last ship?" I asked, looking for a school of fish he hadn't yet scared away. He nodded.

"I was a ship's boy on the *Arnhem*. We came from Holland to transport everyone."

I brought him into the water and demonstrated the bend of my elbow and the spacing of my feet.

"Like this," I said, going through the motions. He squinted, blinking slowly, and seemed to be studying the position of my arm and the twist of my torso, but when I asked him to show it back, he didn't have a clue.

"I'm sorry," he said. "I have forgotten how to sleep."

He sat exhausted in the shade of a boulder, gobbling down the small amberjack I had caught him. He offered me half, but I wasn't hungry. His head lolled from side to side, desperate to succumb to its weight.

"Will you stay? If I just close my eyes?" he said. I didn't answer, but he closed them anyway, rolling onto the sand with the half-eaten fish in his hands.

His lily-pad hat hung over his head and fluttered against his slow and sleepy breaths. I moved his grazed feet into the shade, so they would not burn in the midday sun, and went to get a palm leaf to wrap up his fish. I thought about waking him, to say goodbye and good luck, to tell him to head to the port and wait for rescue. Ships passed every now and then, I was going to say, and perhaps, if someone was looking, they would see him waving on the dock and pick him up. But he was too peaceful to disturb, so I said nothing, and watched the lily pad tremble above his lips.

As I led him over the land bridge at low tide, his small hands digging nervously into my waist, I knew, in the pit of my stomach, that I was making a mistake. I thought of the boy I had buried at Old Grand Port, and all my Malagasy brothers who had suffered at colorless hands like these, but the Governess had already seen us, and was jumping for joy on the beach. When we arrived, she beat her feet and bounced in circles around him.

"This is your friend?" he said, flinching away from her excited pecks.

"This is the Governess," I said, watching him twirl.

With a few deliberate squawks, the Governess spun around and waddled up the beach toward home.

"It's best just to do what she tells you," I said, leading him after her. I had resolved to let him stay with us on Fialofana, just until he was strong enough to go back to Old Grand Port and wait for a ship.

The Governess was pleased to play hostess and gave her

new guest a tour of our home, pointing at various objects with her beak and grunting until she thought he had understood.

"Is she talking to me?" asked Floris, laughing.

"She is trying to show you the kitchen," I said.

"You did all this?" he said, taking in the roof and the bamboo pillars, the mattress and the shelves. I nodded, then reminded him to pay attention to the Governess, who, from what I could gather, was explaining plans for the new extension.

We washed in the stream, using coconut shells to collect the cool freshwater and pour it over our heads. As the grime was carried from his body, the skin that had been hidden under his tattered clothes emerged as white as the moon, and suddenly the rest of him didn't seem so pale by contrast. He turned around and caught me looking, so I sat on a rock and pretended to be busy with my feet. I went in between each toe, and then did it again, feeling his eyes on me. By the time they were cleaner than they had ever been before, a strange warmth was whirling inside me and making my skin feel as if it wasn't mine. But when I looked, his eyes were somewhere else, and the feeling dissolved.

When we climbed out, the Governess was waiting for us next to an aloe plant, nattering away. She had seen me use its leaves to soothe my cuts and motioned for me to snap one off.

"It helps with the stinging," I said, passing it to Floris. I showed him how to rub the soothing gel over his skin, and how to break the leaf to get more. He smeared his grazed feet and sunburned cheeks, delighting in its coolness, and asked me to reach his back and shoulders.

"How did you learn these things?" he said, flinching as I went down his spine.

"We've always known," I said. "We just didn't tell you."

"Me?"

"All of you."

He was silent for a while, and then pulling a blade of grass out of the ground, set it between his thumbs.

"Well, do you know how to do this?" he said, before blowing against the grass and producing a loud, sharp shriek. Back in Madagascar, the other children and I had called to each other just like that, screeching like maniacal birds through the reed, signaling that we were free to play.

"No," I said, meaning to say yes. "Show me."

That night, Floris slept on a bed of palm leaves. I offered him the mattress, but he refused. The Governess spent an inordinate amount of time encircling him with twigs, noisily scuttling in and out with her building supplies and rearranging them until she was satisfied. The jungle chorus, which had tried and failed to send me to sleep the previous few nights, roared on, indifferent. I lay awake, and listened to him breathe.

"How did you find me?" I asked on the beach the next morning. Despite Floris managing to scare away nearly every fish in the ocean, I had caught a wahoo, and was cooking it for breakfast.

"I saw you at the port, but I was scared," he said quietly. "And then when you left, and I knew I was all alone, I was even more scared. So I tried following your footprints. The sea washed them away, of course, so I stopped by a big tree and lived under that. And then one day I decided to keep going, and that's when I saw you, across the water. I thought I could walk across, but the tide was too high, and I don't know how to swim."

I looked at him, entirely out of place in his surroundings, as his lily pad hat flapped in the breeze and glued itself to his face. More than any of the pink men at Old Grand Port, even Tomato Frog, I had never seen someone so unready for where life had dropped him.

"Later, I will show you," I said.

"Okay," he replied.


Standing shoulder deep in the shallows with our feet in the sand, every other wave knocked him off balance and sent seawater shooting up his nose. I held him steady and showed him how to move with the currents, and he soon found his confidence. By the afternoon, after several giant gulps of salty water, he was bobbing about untethered.

He was horizontal the next day. I waded along with him hanging on my waist, kicking his legs. The day after that he was doing it alone.

The Governess observed our lessons from the beach, yapping noisily whenever we strayed too far. One evening, when I found myself distracted by a school of bright red fish, she yelled at the top of her lungs at the sight of Floris disappearing beneath a breaking wave. He quickly surfaced, coughing and grimacing, but it was too much for the Governess, who demanded we call it a day and come in for dinner.

"Will there be someone waiting for you, at home?" I said that night, eyes on the ceiling.

"No," he said from his palm leaf bed. The Governess was asleep beside him, snoring, her head pushed against his armpit. "And for you?"

I thought of my parents, taken when I was eight. "No," I said, finally.

He reached over and pressed my cheek with his finger,

making me flinch. I must've scowled at him, confused, for he drew back, embarrassed, and showed me the squashed mosquito on his fingertip.

When the air turned hot and sticky, I knew it must have been weeks since Floris arrived on Fialofana. Scaling a palm tree to collect the sap from its flower, I remembered the promise I'd made to myself, to send him off to Old Grand Port as soon as he was strong enough.

We downed the sweet drink and got in the water, racing each other up and down, stopping for breaks on the sand when we needed. The Governess sat in between our legs as our chests heaved, and then squawked as we chased each other back in, leaping and splashing until the sun made haste for the horizon and our bodies started to tire. I watched him look out at the burning sunset, his blond head shining above the sparkles in the water, and wondered what it would feel like when everything went back to how it was. He turned to look at me, the golden reflections playing on his face and over his smile, and I hoped it could wait just a little bit longer.

Storm clouds rolled in above, whipping away the heat of the day. Under the pitter-patter of rain on the palm roof, my skin tingled with sunburn and my muscles, loose and languid, hummed with a not-unpleasant ache. Sitting on the mattress with the Governess pressed between us, I squashed a mosquito on his neck as we drank the sap from the palm flower which had fermented and soured throughout the day.

Floris poured some more, and with each sip he let his body sink. I too felt the soft buzz and divine dizziness, falling backward onto the mattress to savor it.

The rain was heavy now, and the jungle chorus ceded to its

roar. Only my thumping heart threatened to pierce it, concerned with something strange and unspoken, racing like it did the day I escaped from Tomato Frog and swam for my life to the shore. Floris's slow breaths whispered through it all, his chest rising and falling like great billows, sweat beading down the sides of his stomach. I closed my eyes and watched the colors swirl in the darkness.

The Governess, never one to give up a cozy spot, wiggled out and waddled off on her own accord, sending a rushing chill into the gap between us.

With every breath it seemed to grow, until the loudness of it became too much to bear. Muted by the rain, I rolled silently onto my shoulder and opened my eyes. He was already there, looking at me, as if he'd heard every thump, every thought. Our chests filled in perfect unison, and as though it was always meant to be, the gap closed, until not a grain of sand could come between us.

There was no need to try to mark the weeks or months. The seasons themselves became our only rhythm, and even those slid into each other with ample warning, giving us little reason to plan ahead. Fialofana provided everything we needed, when we needed it.

It was only when the dry, windy winter came round that I knew it had been a year since the pink men had left. And when the following scorching, humid summer bowed out with its wild storms, I realized it must have been two. Three years meant nothing the next time we huddled together and sheltered from the chilly nighttime gusts, and by the time it was four, I wondered if perhaps I was mistaken, and it had only been one.

Only our bodies gave us clues. I was watching Floris climbing a palm to collect the wine when I noticed he bore little resemblance to the boy I'd found helpless on the beach. His pink skin had turned bronze, his torso, forearms and legs dusted with gold. His chest had risen and hardened under his wide shoulders, and the soft curves of his face had whittled themselves into sharp lines.

I had changed too. As I looked down now, taller than ever, I saw arms and legs lean with muscle. The Governess, however, had just become rounder. Her natural diet of nuts, seeds and fruits had been generously supplemented with our daily catch.

Floris plucked and gutted a couple of wood pigeons he had hunted, careful not to let the Governess see. She, understandably, became agitated when we ate birds. Once I'd caught a red rail, a bird with a striking resemblance to the dodo, and she didn't talk to me for days. As a result, we only had them on special occasions, and we'd decided it was probably my birthday, give or take a few months.*

Outside, a ferocious tempest stirred up the waves and howled through the trees, as though Mauritius was trying to rid herself of invaders all over again. I sat in the reading chair as Floris cooked. After numerous salvage missions to Old Grand Port, our home had become a palace. We had a real bed raised off the ground, a desk for writing, a collection of books to read and shelves to put them in. We had clothes and hats, chairs and maps. We even had a painting of an important-

---

*The red rail was another flightless bird found only on Mauritius. With small wings, stout legs and a long beak, it resembled a dodo, but is much less famous. Like the dodo—and countless other species on the island—the red rail was driven to extinction by the end of the century.

looking pink man, signed by someone called "Rembrandt," which we used as a doormat.

"So you tie knives to your feet?" I asked Floris through the noise, looking up from my book about Amsterdam and the strange customs of its people.

"Blades, yes. So you can go on the ischin slippery dippery," he said, speaking gibberish again. "On the water, when it gets hard in the cold," he added, going off my furrowed brow. "Then you can glide on it, all the way across the town," he said, sliding his feet on the ground and making a swishing noise with his mouth. Even the Governess clicked her beak and shuffled off, bewildered by his nonsense.

The storm relented, so we went for the first swim we'd had in days. The Governess kept watch while we competed to collect a conch from the ocean floor, coming up breathless and empty-handed every time.

Eventually I returned with the prize, cheering as I thrust it in the air. But Floris wasn't watching.

"I got it! Floris!" I shouted, but his attention was elsewhere. I swam to him and followed his stare to a half-submerged crate, floating lazily by.

The emblem slipped up and down above the waterline: VOC. And above it, stamped in plain black letters, a word we both knew.

"*Arnhem.*"

A faint cry carried across the island, the panicked squawks of a hundred birds all at once.

The Governess cawed and pushed off the ground, her thick legs pumping the wet sand.

We went after her, fighting the currents, and made it to the beach. It didn't take long to catch up, her frantic waddling only taking her so far. We sprinted past and rounded the curve, the ruckus becoming louder and clearer. And then came the unmistakable sound of laughter.

A jut of rocks peeled away to reveal the next stretch of coastline. There, four men closed in on a flock of dodos, pinning them against the water. One of the men stepped forward and grabbed a bird, lifting it up by its legs. The helpless creature wriggled and screamed as its friends crowded around it, but there was no hope of rescue. The man gripped its neck and with one firm twist, snapped it. He tossed the body aside and went for another.

We barely noticed the Governess speeding past, squawking her battle cry. Floris chased after her and scooped her up in his arms. She wailed and beat his stomach with her feet, nearly breaking free, but together we were able to restrain her.

The men disbanded, setting free their captives. Some of the dodos scattered, but most of them continued plodding around where they were confined, devoid of the instincts that keep the rest of us alive. With the dead over their shoulders, the men set off along the beach in the opposite direction, disappearing behind the headland.

The last hues of sunset lit our way home, leaving us in darkness the moment we arrived. The Governess nestled down and went straight to sleep, tired from the ordeal. Floris and I got changed into our coats and wordlessly set off into the night.

We found the men on the northern side of Fialofana. There were half a dozen of them, sitting around a fire on the beach. Hanging on a spit, two dodos were roasting in the flames. The men watched them hungrily, the first birds already stripped of all their meat and digesting in their bellies, their bones littered in the sand around them.

Their blond hair, sunburned faces and bouncy accents left no question as to their origin. But they sat in disrepair; faces sunken, bodies emaciated and clothes shredded, like Floris the day he had arrived.

We crept closer, tip-toeing through the undergrowth.

"It's them," whispered Floris, squinting. "It's men from the *Arnhem*. The Captain, Pieter. And Johannes!"

"All of them?" I asked.

"I don't know. Only a few, I think."

We stood and listened to them reminisce about friends they had lost, women they had loved and things they were excited to do when they made it home.

"We should go and talk to them," said Floris out of nowhere.

I shook my head.

"They are here. We can't hide from them forever."

"We should wait!"

"Wait for what?"

"You don't know what they'll do to us," I said.

"They are Dutch. They're harmless."

I gestured, plainly, to the VOC emblem on my arm, to express that this was very much not the case.

"Stay here. I'll talk to them," said Floris, stepping onto the beach.

I pleaded with him not to go, but either my whispers didn't carry or he didn't want to listen.

A boy spotted him and alerted the others. Heads snapped

round, one of the men bolted upright, the others yelped and cursed in surprise.

"Who goes there?" asked the standing man.

"It's okay. I am Dutch. I am one of you," said Floris, holding up his hands.

"You were in the fleet?"* said the standing man.

"I don't know what you mean."

"The *Prins Willem*, the *Maarsseveen*? You were shipwrecked?"

"No."

The men gossiped among themselves. Two of them, Pieter and Johannes, studied Floris with faint recognition.

"Flower. Is it you?" asked Pieter, who was sitting against an old crate looking particularly worse for wear.

"You know him?" asked the standing man.

"Captain. Johannes," said Floris, nodding to both men.

"It is you!" said Johannes. He got up and embraced Floris, laughing.

"Friends, this is Flower," Johannes said to the group. "He was one of us! A ship's boy on the *Arnhem*, many voyages ago." He looked at Pieter, the Captain. "How long has it been—four years now?"

Pieter nodded. So that was it: four.

"He ran away when we left," said Pieter.

Floris took a deep breath. "How did you get here?"

---

*The *Arnhem*, captained by Pieter Anthoniszoon, formed part of a seven-ship fleet sailing from Batavia (present-day Jakarta) to Holland. The fleet was scattered by a violent storm on 11 February 1662 and three ships disappeared without a trace. The *Arnhem* ran aground on a group of atolls and reefs some 120 miles northeast of Mauritius.

Pieter explained how the *Arnhem* was part of a fleet sailing from the East Indies home to Holland. They became separated from the other ships in a terrible storm and were thrown to the rocks, dashing the *Arnhem* to pieces. Some 80 of them escaped on a longboat and rowed for nine days on the open sea. Eventually, God answered their prayers, he said, and delivered them here.

"Where are the others?" asked Floris.

"We separated," replied Pieter. "They are on the mainland."

I pictured all the other Dutchmen finding their way here, to Fialofana, and felt my blood run cold.

"Little Flower!" said Johannes, squeezing Floris's shoulders and marveling at his transformation. "We thought you were dead! How in God's name did you make it all on your own?"

"I am not on my own," said Floris, looking my way. He gestured, summoning me. "Come." All the men's heads turned to search the darkness. I wish I had run, that they had never seen me, but my feet carried me forward, out of the trees and onto the beach. I held my nerve and met their wary stares. And that's when I saw him. The firelight flickering over his small, beady eyes and his round, red face. He swallowed his mouthful and smiled, a trickle of fat dripping down his chin.

"Well, well, well," he said. "If it isn't the Governor of Nothing."

My heart rapped at my chest and nearly ripped it in two. I thought I might faint, but I held out my hand and smiled.

"Welcome to Mauritius."

He stared at me, wet lips twitching, and for a moment I could swear even the lapping waves stopped to listen. And then he slapped his knee and roared. The rest followed suit, laughing until they were breathless. Amid the noise, the Governess wobbled out from the shadows and stood beside me, tilting her head at the curious shapes hanging over the fire.

"And you brought seconds!" said Tomato Frog, reaching for the Governess with his greasy fingers.

Floris stepped forward. I pushed her behind my legs.

"Do not touch her," I said. Again, Tomato Frog's lips began to quiver, but this time no laughter followed.

"I beg your pardon?" he said.

"I said, do not touch her."

The red face got even redder, like a raging furnace fit to explode. He shot up and shoved me to the ground, and in one fell swoop, seized the Governess by the leg. The men all laughed as she dangled, screaming.

Floris rushed to her, but I was already on my feet, launching myself at Tomato Frog. I punched him hard, knocking him backward. The Governess tumbled to the ground and bolted for the trees.

Tomato Frog came back at me, bellowing. I ducked under his fists and threw him down. He grabbed my collar and took me with him.

The men piled on as we wrestled, but I didn't let go. I locked my legs around his waist and pinned his neck, striking him again and again. He kicked and screamed, bloody fingers tearing at my coat and scratching my skin.

More Dutchmen came to his aid. I felt arms wrap around my chest, pulling me away, and swung my elbow to break free. Floris fell backward and clutched his nose. I looked just in time to see his frightened eyes. He fell to his knees and watched, helpless, as blood poured through the gaps between his fingers.

A kick in the head turned everything black. After a few seconds I came to and scrambled to my feet, the men closing in around me, Tomato Frog lying motionless on the ground. I searched for Floris among the blurs, listening for his voice, but everything was lost to the ringing in my ears. I staggered toward the dark tangle of trees and, finding my balance, retreated to the safety of the jungle.

Somehow, I made it home, falling into a heap on the floor. The Governess was nowhere to be seen and Floris hadn't followed me back. I waited in the dark, listening for his footsteps, but they never came.

Thunder rumbled up above. A rolling, growling warning. Quickly, I gathered some supplies—a blanket, a knife, some rope and a roll of canvas—and, after waiting a few more moments for the familiar rhythm of his feet, I ran.

Moonbeams spilled through gaps in the jungle canopy, lighting the way. I made it to the beach and looked out over the crossing, swallowed by the high tide. Tightening the satchel around my shoulders, I pushed off into the choppy water. The campfire still blazed on the other side of Fialofana, highlighting the tops of the palms with its orange glow. I checked to see if the Governess was at the water's edge, watching me go, but the beach was empty. Fighting the currents, I kicked and crawled my way through the foaming waves, and, with only Mauritius herself as my witness, rolled spluttering, once again, onto her shore.

Twenty days passed. I was counting now. After what felt like a lifetime on Fialofana, the vastness of the mainland made me feel small.

The storms gave no respite, and the mosquitos came out in

swarms. I squashed my own but was always too late to get them. Their bites burned on my skin, and I scratched them until they bled.

The days were easier than the nights. There was jungle to navigate, shelter to find, fish to catch and fruit to forage. But in the solitude of darkness, the ache was difficult to ignore. Under my thin strip of canvas, I waited for sleep to rescue me from visions of Tomato Frog's lifeless body and Floris's frightened eyes.

On day 39, a dot appeared on the horizon. I climbed to higher ground to watch it take shape, its masts and sails emerging from the blue. Before long I could see the pink men and their tiny bodies scurrying about on deck. High up on the mainmast, in place of the VOC that fluttered above every Dutch ship I'd ever seen, a red and white one flew.*

The distant shouts of men echoed across the mountain, and down on the beach, a small group started to form, jumping and waving. As the ship drew closer, the little men onboard waved back. The gaggle of castaways, growing in number every minute, fell about laughing and cheering. One of them peeled off, collapsed in the sand and wept. The group on Fialofana would be celebrating too, I realized, and I imagined Floris drunk and happy, dancing around the fire with his friends. He would be gone soon, along with all the other pink men. "Good," I said to myself. "Good."

The light slowly fading, I set up camp on a cliff overlooking the sea. The ship had long disappeared down the coast, toward

---

*The red and white ensign belonged to the English ship, the *Truro*. In May 1662, the *Truro* sailed past Mauritius and came to the rescue of many of the *Arnhem*'s survivors.

Old Grand Port. Below, men relayed information along the beach, all splitting off to inform their colleagues. Two men from Tomato Frog's group met and spoke with messengers from the port before returning in the direction of Fialofana. All around, excited shouts went out. A rallying cry to all lost Dutchmen.

"Onto the beaches! Wait for the ship!"

It was too risky to start a fire, so I got under my blanket and tried to ignore the gnawing inside of me. I listened to the tranquilizing chorus, hoping it would take me, but it was too quiet. Some birds I used to hear on Fialofana were absent entirely and even the crickets seemed languid in their chirps. But that's the only reason I was able to hear it. The shrill note cutting through. I sat up, heart jumping, and it came again.

I crawled around in the dark, searching blindly for a blade of grass. Again and again, the sound pierced the air. I found one, snapped it and placed it between my shaking thumbs.

My short breaths whistled through the reed, sputtering toward one sharp call. Immediately it came back, bright and loud. I blew again, two quick bursts. Three notes returned. The calls coalesced in a racket, ringing back and forth like mad parrots. I blew and blew, trying to purse my lips against my smile. My feet carried me, unthinking, toward the music, with no concern for the roots and rocks in their way. The returning trills got louder and louder until I couldn't be sure they weren't mine. And then we collided in the dark, our arms wrapped around each other, tumbling, complete, to the ground.

The fast-padding footsteps soon followed, hurtling wildly through the undergrowth. The Governess tripped on a branch and came crashing down toward us, rolling like a ball to our side. She scrambled on top of our tangled bodies and danced; bouncing, spinning and squawking.

"Did you see the ship?" asked Floris as we sat on the ledge overlooking the moonlit sea. I nodded. The Governess assembled twigs around us.

"You will go on it?" I said. Floris fiddled with a pebble wedged in a crack in the rocks.

"You could come with me," he said. "We could go to Amsterdam. I spoke to Van de Berg. He said he would help." I'd called him Tomato Frog for so long I had forgotten his real name.

"He's alive?" I said.

Floris nodded. "It's okay. He's a merchant. All he cares about is money," he said. "If I can get some in Amsterdam, he will let you go. I know it."

The Governess plodded happily back and forth, arranging her sticks.

"Just come with me, back to Fialofana. We can talk about it. Nothing will happen, he promised. I made him promise."

In the pit of my stomach I knew, but I rested my head on his shoulder and pretended I didn't.

"Okay," I said.

We reached the crossing a few hours later and, with the water coming up to our shoulders, we waded carefully across, taking it in turns to hold the Governess above our heads. We arrived on the empty beach in silence, the welcoming committee nowhere to be seen.

I carried the Governess through the jungle and held her head as it dangled sleepily underneath her. As we traced the stream and climbed up to our home, I expected to see it ruined, torn down and looted, but everything still stood.

"I told you. We can trust them," said Floris.

Gently placing the Governess down on the bed, Floris and I went to the Dutchmen's camp, following the light of their fire. As the first licks of orange found us, they all jumped up and cheered.

"We thought we were going to have to leave you!" said Pieter, embracing Floris. He turned to me and gripped my shoulder. "You have a good friend here. He was worried sick."

"We all were!" came a bellowing voice from across the flames. Tomato Frog, fatter than ever, staggered over, a smile creasing the red scar along his cheek. "Governor," he said, holding out his hand. "I believe we got off on the wrong foot."

They were all slurring and weaving, drunk on palm wine.* One of the men came to us with a tortoise shell full of it, and poured us both a drink.

"To Flower!" toasted Pieter.

"And the Governor!" yelled Tomato Frog. The men cheered.

The wine soon melted the knot inside my stomach. Sitting on the sand beside Floris, I glanced across the circle at the Dutchmen. Their bodies were smooth now, all the hard lines softened by fat.

Tomato Frog pulled up a chair, one we'd pilfered from his lodgings at Old Grand Port, and sat before us.

---

*Accounts written by shipwrecked sailors, including Volkert Evertsz, who arrived on the island in 1662, described how they whiled away the hours by getting drunk on palm wine, which "tasted so good that now and then we made tolerably free with it, so much so that at times we became somewhat merry . . . Thus we lived daily in a flourishing and careless condition, forgetting even the name of the months and days of the week."

"Flower must think very highly of you, Governor," he slurred, refilling his coconut-shell cup. "You should've heard the things he was offering for your freedom!" He laughed. Floris shifted and sipped his drink.

"Maybe it's the wine, or perhaps it's because tomorrow morning I'll be out of here forever . . . but I have to say, the urge to lash you to death is . . . strangely lacking." He chuckled. "No . . . I think maybe it's because you're a fighter. I've always liked fighters. It's the Dutch spirit." He clenched his fist and pumped his chest. "And that, my boy, is why I'm going to help you."

The men started to sing something rousing and unintelligible, a song they all knew. Tomato Frog spun off his chair, nearly falling, and joined the revelers. Floris looked at me, and in his smile I caught glimpses of a life we'd never live, among the cobbles and towers of Amsterdam. He squeezed my shoulder and, climbing unsteadily to his feet, joined in.

"Schnepel kloppen dop, schloopen glappen toopen top," they sang. The wine made my eyelids heavy, and as I rolled onto the sand, my last thoughts were of the Governess, and of the sounds she would make as we sailed away.

It was his scream that woke me. Somehow the tight coil of rope around my wrists and ankles hadn't done it. Three men rushed to restrain him, wrapping their arms around his body. He kicked and shoved, but they wouldn't let go.

Tomato Frog loomed over me in a lily-pad hat, his large silhouette blocking out the rising sun.

"Good morning, Governor!" he boomed. "Another beautiful day in paradise!"

"You promised!" spat Floris, fighting.

"You see that there," said Tomato Frog, tapping my upper arm with his foot. "That stamp means you belong to me."

He strutted up and down, reveling in the sound of his own voice.

"You've forgotten this, clearly. Running around in your little kingdom. Playing Governor with your . . . friend."

He stopped and grimaced.

"Sorry, I think I just threw up in my mouth. Where was I? Yes! Fortunately for you, slave, I am a businessman. Better yet, a businessman who likes deals. And I would like to make a deal with you, if you are of the persuasion."

"I said I'd get money! Name a price, I'll find it in Amsterdam!" said Floris, hanging exhausted in the Dutchmen's arms.

"Oh, I don't want your money, Flower. Very sweet of you, though. No. I would like something else."

"Name it!" growled Floris.

"Well, I'm a touch embarrassed to admit, friends, that I like my food. Perhaps you have noticed?" He looked down, placing a hand on his bulging belly. "And in my time here on Mauritius I've grown partial to a particular kind of food." He gestured to the other men. "These philistines find it unsavory, though that didn't stop them eating their way through the lot. They're all gone now, you see. I can't for the life of me find one. My last day on the island and all I want, before I sail back home to Holland, is one last mouthful. Is that too much to ask? One last mouthful? Well, I was positively depressed. Inconsolable even. I'd had my final bite without even realizing it. And then I remembered."

He pulled up his chair and, digging his foot under my stomach, rolled me onto my back.

"Bring me my breakfast, slave, and I will see to it you arrive in Holland a free man."

"Never," I said.

"Oh come now, let us bargain first."

"You will not touch her."

"I will do it," said Floris.

"No!" I shouted, twisting to find him.

"We have a deal!" roared Tomato Frog.

"Please, Floris!" I begged.

"If I bring you the bird, he is free," said Floris.

"I will see to it that he is—"

"No. Bird, and he is free."

Tomato Frog folded his arms.

"Fine," he said. "But chop chop, we haven't long!"

Far in the distance, the ship was making its way along the coast, sending out a tender to pick up groups of castaways gathered on the beaches.

Floris pulled himself away from the men restraining him and, glaring at Tomato Frog, set off into the jungle. I looked up at the sky, its pink ribbons curling away, and prayed he wouldn't find her.

Their footsteps soon came. His even and deliberate, hers fast and clumsy, grunting and squeaking as she bounced. They stopped behind the treeline, hidden, and I hoped Floris was changing his mind. I could picture him looking at her, her big head tilting, round body rocking as her feet shuffled to find balance.

Then came her piercing cry. Tomato Frog awoke from his snooze and turned to watch Floris emerge from the jungle holding the Governess by the leg. Her tiny wings flapped as she screamed to her kin. But no rescue party came waddling.

"Excellent! Bravo!" said Tomato Frog, clapping.

"Please don't," I said, throat dry and full of sand. But no one heard.

"Well, don't just stand there," said Tomato Frog, holding out a meat cleaver. "Clock's ticking!"

The ship had collected its last group from the mainland and was heading our way.

"Medium rare, please," said Tomato Frog as Floris took the cleaver. "And if you could squeeze some lemon on it, that would be lovely."

Floris hid guiltily beneath his brow, refusing to look at me. "Where he can't see," he said, voice thin.

"Yes, yes, whatever," said Tomato Frog, batting him away.

Floris walked slowly to the treeline, carrying the Governess like a dead fish in his hand. I saw the shape of him bend down and lay her on the ground. She wriggled, the leaves rustling in a last torpid tussle, her final grunts trailing off. I heard his chest fill, the air quivering in, and then the swing of his arm, the whistle of metal and the sharp thud of flesh and bone.

She hung over the fire, pink and pimpled, the absence of her feathers leaving her half the size. Floris turned the spit and watched the flames scorch her brown.

The ropes around my ankles and wrists were cut. I sat alone and watched the ship sail our way.

"Freedom! Feels good, doesn't it?" said Tomato Frog, standing behind me. I could hear his teeth scraping on her bones, his disgusting tongue churning. "It's disappointing, this one, if that's any consolation." He cast the stripped drumstick into the water. "Was she very old?"

I could have taken him right then, struck him like I did that night. Tear him down, wrap my hands around his neck and push his ugly head into the shallows until he drowned. But instead I looked out to sea, beyond the horizon, and hoped Holland was worth it.

The men assembled as the ship's tender pushed off toward us. One of the boys took a final stroll along the beach and pressed his hands into the sand.

"Mauritius, faithful servant of the Dutch republic!" began Tomato Frog's unsolicited speech. "It is with a heavy heart that I must, once again, bid you farewell. You've been a gracious host, and the catering has been sublime. Thank you for everything, especially the dodos."

He was helped onto the boat, landing heavily on one side and nearly capsizing it. I held back as the men piled on, looking down the beach at the Dutchmen's great gestures of gratitude. Nothing walked the shores now. No dodos gathered, no giant tortoises ambled through. Their bones and shells lay strewn in the sand, tossed aside with no purpose left to serve. The birds that remained, hidden in the weary jungle, withheld their songs. The thunderous chorus reduced to a whisper, a faint echo of what used to be.

"Come on then, boy! Don't dawdle!" barked Tomato Frog. The men were all onboard, waiting. Floris held out his hand to help me up. I climbed in on my own and squeezed into the last empty space beside Tomato Frog.

"You will warn me, won't you, Governor, if you decide to do anything rash?" he teased. "Indigestion always makes me rather irritable."

Floris tried in vain to meet my eyes, but I wouldn't let him. Instead I stared at the rotting boards beneath my feet, and watched the water seep through the cracks.

My heart drummed up my throat as we came alongside the towering *Truro,* whose crew dropped a rope ladder and let it roll into the waves. One by one we scaled it, assembling dazed and disorientated before the captain on deck.

"Welcum unborde da *Truro*, jentalmin! It seamse yuhve had kwite de oordil. Plis mayke yoresells at howm," he bellowed in English, a bizarre language I barely understood.

Sails flying, the ship groaned as it pulled away from the island and rolled sleepily toward the open sea. The captain invited us below deck: "Plis, go end eet." He clocked the Dutchmen's flabby bodies. "Nort dat yew nid it!" he laughed.

I was at the back, last to file past the captain, when he raised his hand to stop me.

"And haw dowee wunt to acommedayt dis won?" he called back to the Dutchmen. Floris stopped. Tomato Frog flashed me a venomous smile.

"Oh, just lock him up with the others," he replied in Dutch.

All was lost to the blur. The captain fell as I smashed past him, my feet pushing across the deck. Then came the tangle of arms, the jostling bodies all around. Floris tried to rip his way through but was quickly buried.

A tempest moved through me now, my muscles burning. Little by little the knot loosened, men falling backward with their ribs crushed and noses streaming. I tore through the last binding arms and charged, head spinning, to the edge.

His eyes found me as I jumped, wide and frightened. And then they were gone, dipping below the hull of the ship as the blue rushed toward me.

The impact snatched my breath away and I surfaced, gasping. Fighting the ship's wake, I kicked into the rolling waves and eventually broke free of its pull.

Fialofana took over just as my body resigned, her currents carrying me to shore. I crawled onto the wet sand and collapsed, eyes drifting over the azure sky until they rolled into black.

It's hard to say how long I spent there, suspended in the darkness. All I know is the sounds came slowly, sticks and twigs dropping near my head.

The lapping waves came next, the wash gliding over the sand, tinkling and fizzing. And then the soft grunts, the brushing of feathers across my skin. I opened my eyes to find her rearranging bits of wood around me, head tilting, beak chattering. When she saw I was awake, she jumped on my chest and beat it with her big cold feet. When I sat up, she skipped in circles around me.

Up at the jungle's edge, where I had heard the whistle of the cleaver, orange-brown feathers spun in the wind, flying off across the sand. A red rail for breakfast.

I held the Governess and sat cross-legged in the foam. The ship was far off now, its great white sails and tiny pink heads melting into the horizon. I wondered if Floris was looking too, watching helplessly as the world dragged me away. Was he, like me, wondering who would squash his mosquitos before they bit him on the cheek?

The Governess leaped from my arms and screeched, her wings flapping as if she might fly. She jumped up and down in the shallows, splashing and squawking until all of Mauritius could hear.

I looked up at the ship fading to nothing. And that's when I saw it. Lost in the blue, riding on the white-tipped waves, his little blond head, swimming toward me.

## THE FACTS

For millennia the volcanic island of Mauritius remained a human-free zone, a tropical paradise teeming with exotic wildlife and plants. Arab ships and Portuguese seagoers alighted there but no one attempted to settle on the island until the Dutch East India Company decided it was theirs in the 1600s. Their aim was to secure a convenient stopping point for Dutch ships navigating the Indian Ocean and to clear the island's abundant forests of ebony wood, a much-prized resource back in Europe.

From the 1640s, they brought in slaves from Madagascar to undertake the back-breaking work of chopping down trees and clearing land for sugar plantations.* They built a garrisoned fort and made several attempts to tame the island, before disease, bad weather and lack of freshwater forced the governor Abraham Evertszoon to call the whole thing off and head home in 1658. Not quite everyone left, though, with the Dutch reporting that two escaped slaves and a ship's boy remained on the island. History doesn't tell us how they fared.

Mauritius was once again visited by people in 1662, this time by survivors of a shipwreck. Various accounts testify to the incident, most famously that of the Dutchman Volkert Evertsz, who had been aboard the Holland-bound *Arnhem* when it, along with numerous other ships, was torn apart in a devastating storm. Escaping on a longboat, Evertsz and around

---

*The slave population grew substantially in Mauritius, particularly during the 1700s under French rule. When Britain occupied the island in 1810, there were approximately 67,000 registered slaves, accounting for around 80 percent of the population.

80 survivors made it to Mauritius on 20 February, hungry and dehydrated after nine days at sea.

The survivors eventually split into groups, with Evertsz and his companions wading out to an islet across from the mainland. "Fialofana," as the young Governor called it, is a real place, though historians aren't certain exactly where it is located. The most compelling evidence suggests it is an islet now called Ile d'Ambre, off the northeast coast of the mainland.

Here, the castaways encountered a group of dodos, Evertsz's description providing the last eyewitness account of the doomed bird living in the wild. Without any natural predators and an abundance of food on the island, the birds showed no fear when confronted by the Dutchmen, flocking to each other in a rather pathetic spectacle: "We drove them together into one place," relates Evertsz, "in such a manner that we could catch them with our hands, and when we held one of them by its leg, and that upon this it made a great noise, the others all on a sudden came running as fast as they could to its assistance, and by which they were caught and made prisoners."

With such easy prey, it's no surprise large numbers of the dodos (and their eggs) were culled, both by the island's human inhabitants and the new species of animals—pigs, rats and the like—brought there by the Europeans.

Evertsz and 19 other sailors were eventually rescued by an English ship in May 1662, while another 34 survivors were picked up by a Dutch ship in November of that year. The Dutch East India company came back to Mauritius in 1664 to give the island one last go, only to pack it all in again in 1710. Five years later, the French had their turn, holding on to it for nearly a century before handing it over to the British in 1810. It would take another 150 years before Mauritius would gain independence.

As for the dodo, there were no confirmed sightings of the bird after the first *Arnhem* survivors sailed away. Some unsubstantiated sightings were reported in the years that followed, but it's thought these were likely the island's lookalike birds, the red rails. These lesser-known creatures eventually joined the famous dodo in oblivion, waddling out of existence by the end of the century. They, along with the native blue pigeons, parakeets, owls, giant tortoises and countless others, learned a little too late that not all human beings are to be trusted.

# 9.

# *The Inimitable Charlie*

In the 1800s, settlers in North America continued their expansion into Indigenous lands in what has been called the Great American Frontier. At the crest of this wave, in the vast and untamed western states, a life of lawless adventure was there for the taking. Ambitious men came to make their fortunes in the gold mines and oil fields, and outlaws terrorized the towns and railroads they built along the way. A thrilling time to be alive if you were a settler, an unfortunate one if you were one of the many Native Americans who lost everything in the name of "progress."

Romantic and blinkered as we are, the Wild West quickly took on a nostalgic sheen, representing ultimate freedom, exploration and adventure. Capitalizing on these aspirational sentiments, former buffalo hunter and Frontier legend Bill Cody, or Buffalo Bill as he became known, created a stage show to keep the dying Wild West alive, and—because this is America—make lots of money in the process. The show opened in 1883 and took the US by storm, selling out Madison Square Garden in record time.

Four years later, Wild West fever reached England, and in 1887, the show was booked for a run in London.

Bill, excited for his first international engagement, brought the entire company with him; humans and animals numbering in the hundreds, including his star horse and faithful Frontier companion, Old Charlie.

While Bill Cody got to tell his version of events in a best-selling autobiography, Old Charlie was not afforded such an opportunity. However, on purchasing the notebooks of a 19th-century horse whisperer at a yard sale in Connecticut in 2006, historians were able to decipher a remarkable transcript attributed to Charlie's understudy, a young horse called Billy, who agreed to share his story for a mint and a head scratch.

Below is Billy's account of that fateful tour, straight from the horse's mouth.

---

"So, we're out in the middle of nowhere and it's the dead of the night, and I hear Bill whispering something, and I think I'm dreaming at first . . . " continued Charlie. He'd already told me this story a hundred times, as with all of his stories, but I knew how much he liked telling it so I opened my eyes wide and said "no way!" in all the right places.

We stood at the bow of the ship, the wind rushing through our manes and making them dance. I licked the delicious sea salt off my lips and looked forward to doing it again.

". . . Now I've been lying down for hours, so I can hardly feel my hooves at this point."

If I had known Charlie would be gone in a year, buried at sea in this very same place, I would've listened to every word.

"'Course we're talking about the '60s here . . . "

Charlie was the real deal, a true Wild West mustang who

spent his youth on the Great American Frontier with his best friend, Bill Cody, at his side. Bill was an all-American man, a rugged 40-year-old hero with flowing locks, an enviable mustache and magnetic personality to boot.*

"... And I look at Bill and go, 'Are you thinking what I'm thinking?' And of course, we're thinking the same thing ..."

Five years before, keen to bottle the essence of his glory days, Bill created the Wild West show. It was a four-hour spectacle like no other, a nonstop extravaganza featuring cowboys, outlaws and chieftains doing war dances, battles, shootouts, raids, hunts and races, all in the safety of the pasteboard plains. The show was a love letter to America. An ode to a lost era where the great American adventure was still alive, all golden and dusty and thrumming with possibility.

"... It was just me, Bill and the sun rising over the horizon. I'm telling you, Billy, you've never seen a horizon like this one."

"Wow," I said at the point in the story when I'd usually imagine myself galloping alongside him. But standing there with the sea spray in my nostrils and the Atlantic Ocean all around me, my mind was busy dreaming of my own adventures. I was much younger than Charlie, just four years to his 20, and I had been his understudy for three of them. All I'd ever known was our ranch in Nebraska and the various arenas we'd performed at. I could run on the ranch, but only up to the

---

*William Frederick "Buffalo Bill" Cody, born in Iowa in 1846, was a former plainsman, US army scout and soldier, and—as his nickname suggests— a prolific hunter of American buffalo. Over an 18-month period, Bill famously slaughtered over 4,000 buffalo, which had once roamed North America in their millions only to be brought to the brink of extinction by the end of the 19th century. Technically speaking, these creatures were bison, but Bison Bill just doesn't have the same ring to it.

fence. And the horizon in the Wild West show was just a painted backdrop, so running into that only got me a telling-off and a headache.

"It was different back then," said Charlie, inhaling loudly. "A different time."

While America might not have been quite as good as it used to be, it was certainly better than anywhere else. One time Bill suggested taking the show to Canada and Charlie didn't talk to him for three days. So, understandably, when the prospect of a tour to England got floated, he was furious.

"I'd rather be melted down into glue!" he cried as Bill led us into our neighboring stables one September evening the previous year. "This is the greatest country on Earth! Why would you want to leave?" Looking out over the ranch, I found it hard to believe anywhere could be better. It was warm and the burning red sunset made all the fields shimmer.

Charlie didn't sign any contracts when the whole enterprise was formed (no hands) so Bill had the deciding vote. Before we knew it, the entire cast and crew, some 500 of us including scores of cowboys, cowgirls, Mexicans and Native Americans,* nearly 200 horses, 18 buffalo, a small herd of Texas Longhorn steers, a handful of donkeys, elk, mules and deer, were on a ship to what Charlie described as "the cesspit of the world."

Most of what I knew about England was from Charlie. It was dark, rainy and miserable, apparently. And the English

---

*Unusually for the time, *Bill's Wild West* provided solid employment and relatively good pay for its Native American cast members—or Indians, as they were more commonly known—and allowed them relative freedom against the backdrop of the US policy of assimilation.

themselves were uptight naysayers, all shuffling around in the mud. They were still bitter about losing America to independence in 1776 and would probably never get over it. Also, they were extremely ugly, like horrible little goblins. But of all England's many faults the absolute worst was the miserable old witch in charge. "Queen Victoria won't rest until we're a colony again. She's obsessed. I read it somewhere," he told me once.

Even though it sounded awful, as we sailed through the fog, I was excited to see the hellscape for myself. I was young and all I'd known my whole life was America, America, America.

It was snowing when we arrived in London, the faint silhouettes of factories and chimneys emerging from the white.

"See what I mean?" said Charlie as we clip-clopped off the ship.

All about the Albert Dock on the River Thames, the little goblins gathered to welcome us. I could see what Charlie had meant, but I didn't find them especially unpleasant to look at. Yes, their skin was gray, and their faces were wonky, and their teeth stuck out in all sorts of directions, but they were smiling and laughing when they saw us, and that can never be ugly. They waved their banners as we came out, gasping and chattering enthusiastically at the sight of all the buffalo, the steers and of course, Bill and Charlie.

My hooves made a satisfying crunch on the snow-covered boards as we moved through the mist and under cranes that creaked over our heads, lifting crates and boxes off ships from faraway lands. As we piled into the train carriages, I wondered how the Londoners ever knew where they were going, considering they all lived in a cloud.

I got a spot by the window and poked my head out to see all the shapes rush by, the iron skeleton of a tall bridge under construction, the looming clock tower at the river's edge and the palace where the old witch lived. I tried to get Charlie to come and look, but he wasn't interested.

We soon arrived at our purpose-built arena in Earl's Court, a huge 20,000-seat stadium looking out over a sand-covered circle, backed with tall, wooden boards. The last sections were getting hoisted up while a team of artists turned cans of red and blue paint into sweeping plains and wide-open skies.

Our accommodation was right next door, a Frontier-style timber village just for the company. I dropped my stuff in the room next to Charlie's and went for a trot through the grounds, along the rows of stables, past the cabins for the cowboys, cowgirls and Mexicans, and through the campgrounds, where the Native Americans erected their tipis.

"Bill, this just won't do," complained the principal buffalo to the boss as I went past. "I expressly asked for a room with a view. It's in my contract!"

Further along, a disapproving elk watched her husband try on some cowboy boots that had fallen out of someone's luggage.

"Look, I'm a gun-slingin' cowboy!" said the husband, affecting a southern drawl.

"Don't you think that's a bit problematic?" asked the wife.

"*Really,* Susan? *That's* the bit you're gonna take offense to?"

As I came to the main entrance, I stopped by a huge poster hanging from the gate. In the middle, a younger Charlie reared up with his hooves in the air, doing his signature mane swish. Bill was on his back, dark and handsome, not yet weathered by the stress of ships and shows and box office reports. The pair of them were magnificent, drafted with such life I half-expected them to leap from the paper and gallop away. Standing on my hind legs and mirroring Charlie's pose, I wondered what I would look like in his place, when he was gone. No sooner had I thought it did my insides run cold. I shook my head wildly until the idea disappeared, and hoped it'd never come again.

"So, you're the new understudy, are you?" I remember him sneering when we were introduced back on the ranch. It wasn't how I had imagined meeting my hero, and I had to abandon my long speech about how I'd dreamed of this moment since I was a foal.

"Yes sir," I said, my hooves trembling.

"Well, you're the wrong color for a start," he said, looking me up and down. It was true; he was a stunning bay and I was a gray. "Must be slim pickings out there."

He asked about my qualifications and previous experience, and I recited, in a very short sentence, my entire CV.

"No time in the Wild West?" he asked.

"No sir."

"Of course not, you're too young."

"But I've heard all about it. I know everything. I can pretend. For the show!"

"Pretend?" he snorted.

"Yes sir, I know all the steps. I'm ready," I said. He stared at me, and although we were the same size, I suddenly felt like a Shetland pony.

"You ever been running so fast your hooves start to tingle?" he said. "When the wind's in your mane, the sun's beating down on your back and all you can smell is the hot desert dust rushing up your nostrils? You ever look out onto the horizon, wonder what's past it and then gallop really, really, *really* far in a straight line to find out?"

I shook my head.

"Then you're not ready. Not even close," he said, spinning on his hooves and trotting away. I stood there in the paddock, feeling the fences close in around me.

"I hope you've brought a good book, kid," said an old mule known as "Suicide Jack," eavesdropping from behind a rock. "Charlie's never missed a show in his life."

Charlie remained frosty for months, but as summer rolled around, he started to thaw, and was blowing friendly raspberries at me by July. As we whiled away our down days in the paddock, I was the only one who hung around and listened to his stories all the way through to the end and then asked to hear them again. When he was done, I would bombard him with questions about the valleys, rivers, rattlesnakes and eagles, and listen, wide-eyed, to the answers.

By September that year, when we weren't working, we would spend every evening alone together in the sun-bleached fields, me lost in his wild tales, him regaling it all with relish. Sometimes, in winter, when Nebraska was frozen over, I would stand by the crack in our stable wall and ask him to do the one about the train robbery, or the one where him and Bill hunted a buffalo the size of a house.

"Well of course, it was a different time . . . " the stories would always start, my cue to close my eyes and float into the prairies.

The rain started falling in London, coming down as a fine mist. Remembering I had promised to help Charlie hang his

American flag, I trotted back toward the stables, practicing his mane swish as I went.

". . . no, it's not a view, Bill! Room with a view means a *nice* view, it doesn't mean any old . . . " continued the principal buffalo, stamping his hooves.

Opening night was upon us before we knew it, and most of the cast had still not recovered from the boat-lag.

"I appreciate you're all still tired," said Charlie as we assembled nervously backstage. "But I need everyone on their A-game."

Some steers next to me ran their lines.

"Even if you think no one can see you," said Charlie, meeting my eyes. "You still need to give it your all." He smiled at me, and I smiled back.

"And I know some of you can get caught up in the moment . . . " said Charlie, side-eyeing a horse called Dynamite. "But let's just stick to the script, please." Dynamite was a serial improviser; he just couldn't help himself.

"And Jack . . . it's called a tight five for a reason, buddy," Charlie said to Suicide Jack, who always brought the house down, if not for a little too long, with his hilarious "obstinate mule" act.*

"Yeah, yeah," said Jack.

---

*The mule Suicide Jack and the horses Unhappy Jack and Dynamite were all real animals who performed alongside Charlie and Billy in *Bill's Wild West* show. Unhappy Jack wowed crowds by jumping six feet into the air with cowboy Buck Taylor glued to his saddle, while the imaginatively named Dynamite earned his name by "going off" at the slightest provocation.

Charlie did a final check of everyone's outfits and confiscated a London constable's hat off one of the donkeys, who thought he might wear it as a funny bit. Charlie explained there were no London constables in the Wild West, and that having one would spoil the illusion.

The bipedal cast members filed in to take their positions backstage. The cowboys adjusted their holsters while the Native Americans straightened each other's headdresses and reapplied their war paint. As the audience filtered into the arena, filling the air with excited chatter, Bill arrived at Charlie's side and checked his saddle and reins, adjusting the straps and making everything trim. He stroked Charlie's head and gave him a scratch behind the ears, just where he liked it. Charlie blew a happy raspberry and bounced on his hooves.

The last audience members found their seats and looked out across the empty stage, illuminated by great electric suns hanging overhead. Waiting in the wings, unsaddled and unbridled, I stood by the eyeholes that were always cut for me and watched as Mr. Richmond, the orator, ascended his small wooden platform and quietened the crowd. All 20,000 spectators stopped and listened as he made his usual introductions, giving them a taste of what was to come. Then came Mr. Levy, the cornet player, tiny in the giant sand circle, who pursed his lips and started to play "The Star-Spangled Banner."*

---

*Half a century before it became America's national anthem, "The Star-Spangled Banner" played in every performance of the Wild West show. Many believe Buffalo Bill's usage of the piece heavily influenced sports games and public events to take on the tradition too, eventually making it so popular and synonymous with America that it was adopted as the official theme tune in 1931.

Backstage, we all fell silent. Charlie cast his eye across the company to make sure we were all closing our eyes and thinking of America. There, crammed in my corner, my hooves sinking into the mud, I was transported to the vast grasslands and endless deserts, hot sun on my skin and dust in my nostrils, galloping with Charlie into infinity.

Mr. Levy played the final note. We listened to it trail off and, opening our eyes, waited for the signal.

Bill's hand dropped, and in a flash, scores of mustangs exploded into the ring in all their colorful glory. The crowd roared as they raced around with the Native Americans on their backs, their quick hooves shaking the stands and kicking a cloud of thick dust into the air. Next came the Mexican horses and their riders, followed by the Frontier cowboys and cowgirls atop their steeds.

After a few loops, with the audience whipped into a frenzy, the parade assembled in the middle and waited for the trumpeter to play the fanfare, heralding the entrance of the stars of the show. I trotted on the spot as Bill and Charlie galloped in at the last, traced the stands and got in position for the grand welcome.

Behind the backdrop, I reared up and swished my mane, just like Charlie did.

"Welcome, ladies and gentlemen, to the Wild West of America!" said Bill to rapturous applause.

One of the cowboys hoisted the American flag above the mass of heaving bodies, and after the customary salute, the company rushed backstage, leaving nothing but wisps of dust and racing hearts behind them.

"We've got 'em," said Charlie as a stagehand wiped the sweat off his face.

"Peter Piper picked a peck of pickled peppers," repeated the principal buffalo, getting ready for his entrance.

With the crowd tantalized, Mr. Richmond announced the beginning of the story, in which Native Americans lived their primitive lives in the wilderness, before the settlers came and fixed everything. Two chieftains made a sign of peace and then celebrated with their tribes, dancing in all their beads and feathers, and then WHOOSH! an enemy tribe swooped in for a surprise attack, sparking a thrilling and bloody battle.

Next up was the "emigrant train scene" where bright-eyed settlers made their way through the plains in their heavy wagons, singing songs and dreaming of a better life over the horizon, only to be pounced upon by more pesky tribesmen.* This rivalry presented itself in many different nail-biting scenarios, most famously in the Deadwood Coach scene. The legendary carriage, used for years on the real Frontier, rolled into the arena full of passengers, only to be descended upon by warriors. The coach whizzed around the ring at breakneck speed, trying to shake the pursuers who galloped alongside on their mustangs, and then at the last moment, when all seemed lost, Bill, Charlie and their comrades swooped in to save the day, sending the baddies packing.†

---

*As the *Telegraph* reported in 1887: "The Indians succeed for a time but are ultimately repulsed by the brave cowboys, headed by the indefatigable Buffalo Bill . . . and the fancifully attired Indians are supposed to be left dead on the field." In reality, Indians rarely attacked wagon trains, but audiences nonetheless lapped up Buffalo Bill's version of the Wild West in which noble cowboys tamed animals and fought Indian "savages."

†The battered Deadwood stagecoach once traveled between Cheyenne, Wyoming, and Deadwood, South Dakota. Purchased by Buffalo Bill, the real coach formed a key part of the dramatic reenactment, which was im-

Strangely, the Native Americans were always quite friendly in real life, and Bill, who had fought some of the same cast members back on the actual Frontier, got on with them like a house on fire. Once I'd asked the principal buffalo how this could be and he said, "It's theatre, darling . . . best not ask too many questions."

Another time I asked Charlie if the Native Americans got up and ran off after being killed in the real Wild West, like they did in the show, and he just said he couldn't really remember and changed the subject.

The show wasn't all fighting, though. There was Charlie's dance interlude, Bill's famous buffalo hunt, and a segment where cowgirls Annie Oakley and Lilian Smith shot impossible targets out of the air.* The Native American and Mexican horses raced each other around the ring, "King of the Cowboys" Buck Taylor lassoed Texas Longhorns, stuntman Mustang Jack jumped clean over a horse with dumbbells in his hands and Suicide Jack left everyone in stitches with his not-so-tight tight five.

After nearly four hours of thrills, the show ended on an

---

mortalized by Doris Day in *Calamity Jane*. Other iconic scenes included the Pony Express, which depicted the horse-mounted riders who would deliver mail across the US, an arrangement which lasted for just 18 months from 1860–61. This new method of communication was considered revolutionary at the time, but within a year, telegraph poles were erected across the continent, and pony-power messaging fell out of vogue.
*Annie Oakley and Lilian Smith (born 1860 and 1871 respectively) were legendary sharpshooters, who performed an array of trick shots and stunts, with Oakley famously shooting cigarettes out of her husband's mouth. Bucking the trend of misogyny at the time, Oakley's talents were rewarded with the show's highest salary after Bill himself.

epic battle between the Native Americans and the settlers, won at the last second by Bill and Charlie, who did a victory lap of the arena and basked in the applause.

As everyone floated out of the opening show, high on adrenaline, I hung back, as I often did, and practiced Charlie's scenes alone. It was quiet now and I could concentrate, going over the steps under the electric lights flickering overhead.

I ran backstage and galloped on again, tracing the empty stands and kicking my hooves in the air. I ran after the buffalo, remembering the cadence of Charlie's hooves, and chased the fleeing chieftains, rearing up and whinnying when he always whinnied.

"BILLY, BILLY, BILLY!" screamed the ghosts from their seats. "BILLY, BILLY, BILLY!"

"Time to clock off, kid," came Suicide Jack's voice from afar. I turned around to find him standing at the entrance, half in shadow. "We're passing around a saltlick in the green-stable, if you're of the persuasion? It's good stuff."

"I've got to practice," I said, "but thank you." Jack turned to leave but didn't.

"He'll never let you take over, you know," he said.

The ghosts were silent now, lost to the harsh buzzing of the lights.

"I don't want to take over," I said. It was true, mostly. "But he gets tired, and I have to be prepared, for when he needs a rest."

Jack looked down at his hooves and sighed.

"He's not going to rest, kid. Why do you think he never lies down?"

"It's so he's always ready," I said. "In the Wild West, you've got to always be ready."

Jack shook his head.

"It's because he knows he might never get back up."

I thought back to the ranch and how Charlie would stand over me and the younger mustangs as we lay in the sun on our days off. I could tell by the way he looked at us that he wanted nothing more than to feel the earth take his weight, and let his weary old limbs sink into the soft grass.

"And if he doesn't get back up . . . well, there goes the show, there goes my paycheck, there goes the Wild West," said Jack.

A cold gust whipped through the desolate stands, spinning into the ring and making me shiver. The electric suns, fizzing and crackling over my head, did nothing to warm my skin. They poured their blue, lifeless light out across the sand and fell flat upon the painted plains.

Charlie didn't rest, and under his stewardship the show took London by storm. Rave reviews came pouring in. The *Kensington News* wrote that audiences were left "spellbound" and the *Illustrated London News* called our show "the most remarkable ever seen in this country." We were a hit and before long, you couldn't beg, steal or borrow a ticket.

The sun came out, which surprised me because Charlie said they didn't have one in England. It was a different kind to the sun back home; softer, further away and nowhere near as red. And it never stayed for long. The air was still cold, but not as biting as it had been when we arrived, and some of the trees in the Frontier village were even starting to blossom, their pink petals standing out against the wood and the mud.

Four days after opening, Charlie and I finished our lunch of steamed oats and went to the green-stable to chill out before the matinee. He was halfway through the story about him and Bill traveling 100 miles in 10 hours through the prairies for a

$500 bet, and was just getting to my favorite bit, when the donkey with the constable's hat poked his head around the door.

"Boss, you're gonna wanna come and see this," he said.

We followed him outside to the public entrance where gossiping mules stood around a small sign fixed to the gate. "Today's performances canceled," it read.

"Shut down already, gentlemen?" chuckled a sardonic English horse called Sebastian who turned up in the village to bother us one day and never left. His voice was so silky his sentences came out in one syllable. "Suppose it's back to the colony for you lot!"

There wasn't any time to ask questions. The impatient stagehand came out of nowhere to hurry us all along, herding us toward the green-stable. It all happened so quickly I barely noticed Charlie was no longer by my side.

Inside the green-stable, whispered rumors and half-baked theories ricocheted off the eaves. A small gang of steers reckoned we'd been shut down by a rival production because we were simply too good, and one pale-looking elk thought immigration had finally tracked her down after a lifetime on the run.

I pushed through the crush and poked my head out of a window. Out on the main street, the principal cast were assembling neatly, as if for a photograph. The chieftains sat on their mounts in full dress, resplendent feathers shivering in the breeze. The cowboy band stood with their instruments at the ready, while Annie Oakley, Lilian Smith, Mustang Jack and Buck Taylor straightened their collars and tidied their hair. At front and center, Bill sat astride Charlie, his head held high. Charlie's ears reached for his tail, hooves twitching.

A heavy silence fell upon the company as a black horse trotted up the road toward them, carrying on its back a very serious-looking man in a black coat and top hat. The austere pair stopped a few yards from Bill, turned sideways at the edge of the road and froze. Save for the feathers and the hair and twitching brims of cowboy hats, all was still, until one of the chieftain's mustangs lost his balance and stumbled ever so slightly out of line.

"Careful now," sneered the plummy-voiced black horse with a precautionary side-eye. The chieftain pulled on his reins and steadied his mount.

"Who is it?" asked the principal buffalo crammed in behind me.

"What's going on?" asked the mule crammed in behind him.

The padding of hooves and rattle of wheels brought with it an ornate black coach, driven by two handsome chestnuts. It whizzed down the road, steered by a tiny man dressed in red and flanked by half a dozen more horses and riders.

"It's President Cleveland!" said an elk, sparking a surge of delighted chatter.

The leader of the cowboy band raised his trembling hand and gave the signal to play. The first few unsteady notes of the British national anthem fell out of their instruments, but as the coach swung past, the tiny man shook his head.

"Next one," he said from the side of his mouth. The anthem tumbled away. The band leader turned bright red.

Heavier hooves came, and past the green-stable rattled another coach, larger, blacker and less ornate, pulled by two huge stallions as dark as the night. Behind, four more horses followed with their surly riders. All in black.

"Who died?" joked Suicide Jack, squashed in beside me.

The band started up again, their underrehearsed anthem coming out rushed and messy. Bill cleared his throat. Charlie shuffled his hooves. I squeezed forward for a better view and, as the coach rolled past, I could just about make out the stern silhouette in the window: a round face, prominent nose and disappearing chin. But within moments the visage was gone, curving past the assembled cast and off toward the arena.

"It's the Pope," said Suicide Jack with absolute certainty. "Swear to God, it's the Pope."

I rushed out as soon as the green-stable doors opened.

"Excuse me, why wasn't I invited to stand with the principal cast?" complained the principal buffalo to the stage manager. "I *really* should be kept in the loop with these kinds of things."

I weaved my way through the throngs and found Charlie behind one of the stables, giving Bill an earful.

"You *cannot* be serious!" he said, flaring his nostrils and kicking his hooves into the mud. "I let you have the tour, Bill, but I will NOT let you have this!" Bill held on to his bridle and tried to pacify him.

"C'mon, boy, c'mon," he said.

"Have you gone mad? What were you even *thinking*? Does 1776 mean *nothing* to you?" he went on.

"Easy boy, easy! What's the matter?"

"What's the matter? What's the matter?! I'll tell you what's the matter . . ."

The stage manager appeared with his whip and bad attitude and pushed me toward the arena with the rest of the cast.

We funneled in behind the towering wooden backdrops where I shoved my way through the bodies to see if Charlie was coming, but Mr. Richmond was already stepping up to his platform and clearing his throat.

A quiet panic stirred through the company as, row by row, everyone realized Charlie wasn't there. He had never missed a performance, not once. Lame or sick, he was always there.

"Okay, boy," said Bill, swinging a saddle onto my back. "It's you and me today." The mustangs around me gasped and took a step back, clearing a circle.

". . . What?" was all I managed as Bill fastened the straps around my chest.

"What do you mean we're doing a show without Charlie?" scoffed the principal buffalo. "That's impossible!"

"This is going to be a disaster!" said Suicide Jack.

Hysteria took hold as Bill slipped on my bridle.

"I think there's been some kind of mistake," I said, finally. But he was already on my back, squeezing my sides with his legs and shoring up the reins.

Mr. Richmond's introductions trailed off all muted and scrambled, as if spoken in another language. And then came Mr. Levy's "Star-Spangled Banner," ringing through the near-empty stands. I tried to close my eyes and think of America, but the swirling behind my eyelids just made me dizzy, so I stared ahead and took some deep breaths.

Bill raised his arm to give the signal, and just as the last lonely note carried itself away, dropped it. The company whooshed past me, thundering into the arena for the opening parade. Round and round they went, the roar of hooves shaking the pasteboard backdrop and rattling my bones.

"Ready?" said Bill. The shaking stopped as the company fell into formation before the audience. I waited for the sound of the trumpet and felt a fire rush up inside of me, making my lips tingle. Finally, the fanfare sang and out we flew, my veins burning, the electric air thick with dust. We arrived in the middle, the company behind us. I reared up and kicked my front hooves, just as Charlie always did.

"Welcome, Your Majesty, to the Wild West of America," said Bill, piercing the silence.

"Pleased to be here," came a tiny voice from behind the cloud.

Mote by mote, the dust before us dissipated, revealing a little old lady sat front and center of the royal box, four fancily dressed companions about her. Either side of the velvet-draped, gold-trimmed dais, 20 or 30 more top-hatted men and pale-faced women watched from the benches. Behind them, poised and sincere, rows of police officers looked out from the brims of their funny helmets.

Bill bowed deeply on top of me, and the rest of the company quickly followed suit. Queen Victoria* gave an almost imperceptible nod of acknowledgment and cast her gaze along the lines of feathers and manes and hats. Charlie had always told me the Queen looked like a depressed frog, sneering, joyless and forever bored. And while I agreed with the frog part, her eyes that day were glimmering with childlike curiosity.

"For peace and friendship to all the world!" came the booming voice of the standard bearer, who, as in every performance,

---

*Victoria (1819–1901) was Queen of the United Kingdom of Great Britain and Ireland from 1837 until her death. Following the death of her husband, Albert, in 1861, she famously entered a state of mourning, dressing in black for the next 40 years, and was rarely seen in public. But even the Head Goblin herself couldn't turn down the chance to see Buffalo Bill in the flesh. Thrilled by what she saw, she invited him back to England to perform at Windsor five years later.

lifted the Star-Spangled Banner above his head and drew great circles with it in the air.

I could tell by the way Bill's legs squeezed around me, and how my reins fell slack, that he wasn't expecting her to stand. The wooden benches creaked as her entourage, taken by surprise, hesitantly followed. The men removed their top hats, the ones with medals and epaulettes saluted, and the Queen herself bowed her head.

A triumphant yell flew up from the company. The cowboys launched their hats into the sky. I reared up, hooves kicking, and felt Bill's heart thumping through my sides. I looked around, hoping Charlie was watching. If only he had seen it. The Queen of England saluting the Star-Spangled Banner. He wouldn't have believed his eyes.

Bill reckoned the rest of the show was the best we had ever done, and while there might not have been a deafening crowd, my ears rang as though there had been.

Even without Charlie there to conduct it all, every horse, steer and buffalo performed at their very best. I followed his cues without one misstep and swished my mane in all the right places.

It wasn't until the end, when we were all presented to Queen Victoria, did I realize quite how convincing I had been.

"And this must be the famous Charlie?" said the Queen, touching the side of my nose.

Bill paused and watched her admiring eyes run down my neck and along my body.

"The one and only," he said.

Everyone headed to the green-stable to celebrate, a palpable buzz carrying us there. I tried to peel away to look for Charlie but got swept along with the crowd.

"Kid, you were something else!" said Suicide Jack, nudging my flanks. "I thought there was only one Charlie, but goddammit, there's two!"

"Incredible show, gentlemen!" said Sebastian, the lingering English horse, trotting eagerly along the fringes and trying to get my attention.

"Sorry, sorry, can we all just take a minute? Like, Billy . . . what the hell?" gushed a vibrating deer with pupils bigger than her eyes.

Bill had organized warm oats and saltlicks in the green-stable, and everyone piled in to get the after-party started. The room was loud with excited chatter as we all tried to process the unexpected turn of events.

"But where was Charlie?" asked the principal buffalo. "Is he okay?"

Pushing through the crush, I slipped out and went to find him.

His stable door was closed when I arrived, and there was no answer when I called to him. The fizzing inside me was all gone now, replaced by an unpleasant heaviness that pulled me into my stable and onto the floor. I pressed myself against the wall and tried to peek through the cracks, but all I saw was black.

"Charlie?" I whispered. "Are you okay, Charlie?"

The faint sounds of celebration carried over from the green-stable. The buffalos were singing a sped-up version of "God Save the Queen."

"Charlie?" I said, a bit louder. His breathing had gotten noisier recently, and I could hear the air filling and emptying his lungs. "Don't worry, Charlie, I think we pulled it off! And I did all the right steps."

The breathing stopped.

"Well, at least now we know for sure," he said, plainly.

A numbness crawled out of my stomach and into my chest. The words got stuck in my throat.

". . . Know what?" I finally managed, without wanting to hear the answer. The air whistled in and out of his nostrils.

"That you're not ready," he said, moving away from the wall.

The next day, Bill came to our stables before the matinee to find Charlie standing outside, ready to go.

"Boy, am I glad to see you," he said.

Off they went, without so much as a glance my way. I waited for the stage manager to come and get me, and followed him, long faced, through the arena and into position, behind my eyeholes.

Charlie didn't miss a show after that. Even when Queen Victoria's obnoxious son, the Prince of Wales, brought along a whole busload of European kings and queens for another private performance, Charlie gritted his teeth and gave it his all. As I watched him out there, burning bright, I felt embarrassed at ever having thought I had done him justice. How foolish to believe I could shine like him and hold the crowd in the palm of my hoof, like he did.

He stopped telling me stories at breakfast and through the wall separating our stables and spent most of his time alone. When we were together, he would ask me how I'd slept and what I thought the weather was going to do. As he politely said "good morning" and things like "Indian summer," I longed to be back on the ranch with him, smelling the hay drying in the barn and listening to a tale I'd heard a thousand times before.

"What's going on with you two?" I overheard Suicide Jack ask him one evening in the green-stable.

"Who, Billy?" he said, looking over at me. I was pretending to listen to the principal buffalo and his understudy discuss *Hamlet*. "Nothing. Why?"

One day in late summer, when Charlie had been struggling with his knees, Bill came to my stable and started saddling me up. I blew unhappy raspberries and stamped my hooves until he stopped, by which time Charlie was standing outside, looking the very picture of youth.

"I just don't want to wear you out, old boy," Bill said, going over to Charlie and getting him ready.

But Charlie was getting worn out. On stage, he soared like he was three, but he paid for it afterward. When the crowds were gone, his aches and pains would send him to his stable wincing.

"It's just this darned leg!" he would say whenever someone raised concern. "Must've twisted it on something."

In October, after more than 300 performances and 2.5 million tickets sold, our run in London came to an end, but at Bill's behest, we continued touring England. We shivered through the harsh winter, during which half the Native Americans quit and sailed home, and braved dark and depressing runs in Birmingham and Manchester.

"Bill, this is barbarous!" complained the principal buffalo as we checked into our accommodation in Salford.

Our farewell performance took place on a muddy football pitch in Hull the following May, where, without our pasteboard scenery and circle of sand, we tried to conjure the spirit of the Frontier for an enormous crowd of eager Englishmen. It was there, hooves caked in mud, that Charlie stumbled and missed a cue. It had never happened before, and took us all by surprise, not least Charlie, who staggered through the rest of the scene in a daze, forgetting to rear up for the audience as he bounded after the fleeing chieftains. The show finished without any more hiccups and the crowd cheered and applauded as loudly as ever, but as we came on for the encore, Charlie didn't do his signature mane swish, and I knew something was very wrong.

He disappeared as soon as Mr. Richmond closed out the show, quicker than I could follow him. I ran ahead of the rest of the company and looked for him in the stables, but he wasn't there. I called out his name and went along the edges of the stadium, galloping through the evening drizzle that had descended over us and hastened the sunset, but he didn't answer. Going back to the stables, I found them empty, the mustangs, buffalo and mules nowhere to be seen.

My hooves quickened along the dirt tracks as I called out for the others, squinting through the rain and the gloom, looking for someone, anyone.

"Over here," came Suicide Jack's voice from across the way. I ran after it and found, in a muddy clearing beside the road, the company standing in a circle under a huge poster for the Wild West show.

"Nothing to see here, folks," said the donkey in the constable's hat, trying to move everyone along.

Jack stepped out and smiled at me sadly, softly. I pushed through the bodies, flicking my rain-soaked mane out of my eyes and felt my heart beat heavy and thick. There was Charlie, under the cold flicker of an electric floodlight, looking up at the poster, lying down.

I went to him and let my legs fold under me, falling silently by his side. Above us, the enormous poster bubbled against the soot-covered bricks and peeled at the corners, but Charlie and Bill still loomed magnificent in the middle, as radiant as ever.

"I might need you to fill in for me . . . when we're back home. Just a couple days a week," said Charlie, raindrops ringing his eyelids and dripping down his face.

"Are you sure?" I asked.

"Just for a few days, while I get rested."

I followed his stare back to the poster and watched its corners flutter in the breeze, a stretch of prairie peeling away from the black bricks beneath.

"What if I'm not ready?"

The drizzle collected in beads on Charlie's head, making him sparkle in the electric sun.

"Help me up," he said, lungs rattling. Pushing myself onto my feet, I looked out at the somber faces and asked, wordlessly, for their help. Jack came first, trotting over to put his head against Charlie's side. One by one, the buffalo and the mustangs followed, then the mules and the elk and the steers, pushing in to lend a snout or a horn.

"'Course, it was different back then," said Charlie a year before we left for London, back on the ranch. The sun had fallen below the hills and painted the plains pink. I was already dreaming about my trip to England and trying to picture the little goblins that lived there, so just nodded along to Charlie's story and said "wow" in all the right places. "Back then, there was no yesterday. Hell, there wasn't even tomorrow. The sun came up and the sun went down, but it was always today. Have I had too much saltlick? Anyway, all I'm saying is, forget the rest of it, forget the steps, *that's* the Wild West. That's what it's all about."

It was in the early hours that I felt his nose nudge my side. Our boat was leaving Hull that morning to make the long journey home and, stirring in the straw, I wondered if I had slept through my wake-up call. But it was still dark outside, and I could hear everyone's snores carrying through the stables. I opened my eyes to find Charlie standing over me.

"Come," he whispered.

Wearily, I stood, feeling the blood return to my legs. I blinked the sleep out of my eyes and followed him outside.

Off we went, across the courtyard and through the gate, my hooves sticking to the wet mud. I followed his fuzzy outline, black against the bright stars that had gathered in a great streak across the sky.

The stables grew small as we walked, and soon they were lost entirely. Further we went, along the roads and through the fields, until the mud turned to pebbles beneath my hooves, and the soft roar of the ocean carried from far away. Before us, left gleaming by the receding tide, quicksilver sands stretched to infinity, melting into pink and orange slithers that glowed softly at first, and then threatened to catch alight.

"Ready?" said Charlie, breathing in the salty air. I drew a straight line from my hooves, up and out across the beach, into the horizon and far away.

"Ready," I said.

## THE FACTS

In the late 19th century, Buffalo Bill's Wild West show was the hottest ticket on Earth. Long before filmmakers immortalized the Great American Frontier in their spaghetti westerns, Bill's spectacle thrilled audiences, stunned reviewers and delighted even the most surly of monarchs.

Bill, whose full name was William Frederick Cody, was a former plainsman, US army scout, buffalo (bison) hunter and legend of the American West. A superb horseman, he had ridden Charlie, a half-blood Kentucky horse, across the American plains for some 13 years, during which time Charlie had proven himself—in Buffalo Bill's words—"of almost human intelligence, extraordinary speed, endurance and fidelity."

When the American Exhibition was organized in London as part of Queen Victoria's Golden Jubilee celebrations, Bill's show was chosen to represent the very best of America. It completely overshadowed the other exhibits, which are all too boring to mention, and whipped London into a frenzy. It wasn't long before Wild West fever found its way to Buckingham Palace, with the Queen herself requesting a private performance on 11 May. Rarely seen in public, Victoria couldn't wait to see what all the fuss was about and found herself utterly captivated by the show, excitedly writing in her journal: "An attack on a coach, and on a ranch, with an immense deal of firing, was most exciting, so was the buffalo hunt and the bucking ponies . . . " She described Buffalo Bill as a "splendid man, handsome and gentleman-like in manner." (Victoria was often rather taken by outdoorsy men, and the sight of Buffalo Bill surrounded by chap-wearing cowboys and half-naked Native Americans astride magnificent mustang horses was probably more than a little exciting for her.)

Significantly, it was also reported that the Queen stood and bowed when a horseman waved the American flag above his head, marking the first time since the Declaration of Independence that a British sovereign had acknowledged the Star-Spangled Banner. Curiously, reports disagree as to the color of Bill's famous steed that day. The *Washington Post*'s report described Colonel Cody's "gray horse Charlie" wowing the Queen, while other souvenirs from the American Exhibition describe the "dark bay (brown) gelding." It is possible then, as recorded in this version of events, that Billy stepped into the leading role that day.

A subsequent Royal Command Performance on 20 June attracted an impressive number of crowned heads from Europe, including four kings and a smattering of princesses and princes. Queen Victoria's eldest son, the Prince of Wales (wearing a ridiculous white top hat), lorded over the event, stopping and starting the show at whim, with members of the royal party examining Annie Oakley's gun and even clambering on the Deadwood Coach so they could be "attacked" by Native Americans in a volume of smoke.

Behind the excitement of the performances, though, was a darker truth. Typically, during the show, the Native Americans might seem to be winning, only to be brought down by the "brave" cowboys, just as American settlers killed and relocated millions of Native American "savages" as they expanded their territory westward. Buffalo Bill himself was famous not only for slaughtering buffalo but for scalping Native warriors in the Plains War of 1876, all of which he glorified in his later stage shows. He insisted, however, on hiring real Native warriors to perform in the show—including Red Shirt, a Lakota chief who was presented to the Queen—later adding Mexicans, Zula warriors and various other peoples to the cast. The show was, of course, a grotesque distortion of the realities of life in the Wild West, particularly for Native Americans, although Cody himself claimed he respected the Indigenous people, regarding them as friends and insisting he pay his Native performers a fair wage. He even eventually came to regret the massacre of buffalo that had given him his stage name.

The audience, including Queen Victoria, were nonetheless enthralled by the sight of the Native American performers whirling around at full gallop, chieftains resplendent in striped blankets, American Indian women in traditional dress and Red Shirt eagle-feathered from head to toe. As one newspaper report put it: "The whole thing comes and goes like a lightning flash, and the spectator, dazzled, gazes over the wild, vacant enclosure, uncertain whether what he has just seen was reality or a dream."

After a year in England, the company began the long journey back to the United States. They were halfway through their voyage across the Atlantic when Old Charlie unexpectedly became ill and, with Buffalo Bill by his side, passed away. Surrounded by the crew of *Bill's Wild West*, Charlie was lowered slowly into the ocean as the band played "Auld Lang Syne," while a heartbroken Bill made the eulogy:

Old fellow, your journeys are over. Obedient to my call, gladly you bore your burden on, little knowing, little reckoning what the day might bring, shared sorrows and pleasures alike. Willing speed, tireless courage, you have never failed me. Ah, Charlie, old fellow, I have had many friends, but few of whom I could say that I loved you as you loved me. Men tell me you have no soul; but if there is a heaven and scouts can enter there, I'll wait at the gate for you, old friend.

After Charlie's death, Billy finally trotted into the spotlight as Buffalo Bill's principal steed. Posters, banners and advertisements were redesigned to feature the handsome gray in place of Old Charlie and, over the following four years, Billy became a star in his own right, appearing in more cities and before more important people than even his beloved predecessor.

Sadly, his star burned fast and bright, and in 1892, after returning from a second smash-hit European tour, Billy clip-clopped off the ship and immediately collapsed. With no previous signs of sickness recorded, it is safe to assume his heart simply stopped beating.

As for William Cody, in 1917 he finally lay down at the age of 70, and never got back up. Many said the Wild West died the very same day, and with it the true spirit of freedom, exploration and adventure. But that is easily disproven. Like young Billy, one simply has to go really, really, *really* far in a straight line to experience it for oneself.

## 10.

# *The Wheat Field Marshal*

Thirty years after her death, the sun still hadn't set on Queen Victoria's expansive empire, but cracks on the world stage were beginning to show. After the Great War (which wasn't all that great), the Great Depression (again, not that great) came along to rub everyone's noses in it. Economies crashed, populations starved and political tensions bubbled toward an inevitable sequel to the big fight we swore would be our last.

No one's plight could compare, however, to that of the farmers of Campion, Western Australia, in 1932. Quite uninvited, emus were marching into their fields and helping themselves to the crops. With a devastating harvest on the horizon, the farmers called on the government for assistance. A major and two artillery soldiers were deployed armed with 10,000 rounds of ammo and a couple of machine guns. They arrived in Campion confident they'd be able to quickly annihilate the ballooning population and be home in time for tea. But the giant flightless birds, of course, had other ideas.

Much of the detail of this conflict was thought to have been lost to time, but in 2008, an emu appeared on *Antiques Roadshow* with a top-secret ledger. In it, as well as keepsakes and watercolors, were the war diaries of her great-great-great-great-great-great-great-great-great-great-great-great-great-great-great-aunt, Field Marshal Matilda Montgomery.

Below are some declassified hand-picked entries, made public for the first time.

---

## DAILY REPORT: 31 October 1932

Bored, bored, bored at 0900 hours. I was enduring yet another monotonous peacetime morning in the Campion fields when Patricia suggested I join her in painting the endless rows of wheat, but I haven't the patience for watercolors. I remember saying to the old girl, "I wish something interesting would happen," and then, quite out of nowhere, a farmer charged us with a pitchfork. We made a tactical retreat, abandoning Patricia's easel, and regrouped by the tree that looks like her fifth husband Ron. Patricia told me to be careful what I wished for.

Sensing an uptick in hostility, I reluctantly (Patricia says there was nothing reluctant about it) assumed the role of Field Marshal of the Emus.* I immediately enlisted Patricia as my general, to which she responded, "Yes, dear."

0930 hours. I sent for Colonel Madge, our peace envoy, to discuss an emergency treaty.

Colonel Madge left for the farmer's house to broker peace

---

*Among a group of emus, there often appears to be a leader, an enormous bird who keeps watch while the rest of the mob eat.

at 1100 hours, but was screamed at and pelted with shoes on arrival. She was forced to return before any terms could be discussed.

Convened a council to discuss further action at 1420 hours. We concluded, unanimously, that the fields are too good to give up on. Most of us have traveled many hundreds of miles to be here, so surrender is simply not an option.

I've assembled a delegation to meet with the regional farmers in the AM. We shall try once more to find a peaceful solution to our cohabitation, and if that fails, I will have no choice but to declare a state of war.

General Patricia and I supped on wheat and retired at sunset. The general commented that I was seeming very chipper. I reminded her that war is serious business, and to be chipper in its midst would be extremely inappropriate. However, on further pushing, I confessed I hadn't felt so alive in years.

## DAILY REPORT: 1 November 1932

Our peace delegation left this morning at 0830 hours and returned 15 minutes later covered in manure. Our Ambassador for Sapiens and Reptiles tried her best to engage in civilized discourse but the farmers, unsurprisingly, were unable to muster suitable manners.

At 1415 hours I visited the eucalyptus chambers for a chinwag with Kathy, Koala of Law, and lifelong friend.

Despite claiming they own the crops *and* the land, Kathy, citing Clause 7 of the Animal Rights Act, told me no one owns anything, we are all just momentary fizzes of consciousness manifesting in disintegrating bags of electricity, briefly visiting a world that has been here long before we arrived and will continue to be here long after we leave. Asked Kathy if she was having a stroke and she said, "No, but the gist of it is, the fields are fair game."

I signed the relevant articles at 1630 hours. We are now, regrettably, at war. ~~Spiffing!~~

At 1700 hours, the war council convened to discuss next steps. It was decided a full and unwavering advance is required, engaging all local farms simultaneously.

The plan is to descend upon each of the farmers' most prized fields and lay waste to their crops. Provoked, the farmers will have no choice but to leave their homes and come running, at which point our flanks will circle round and imprison them. With them captured and outnumbered, we will demand a treaty, enacting the Free Graze Convention in perpetuity.

At 1745 hours a crack team of echidnas cut off access to the region by blocking the road with twigs. It should hold off any external interference for the next day or two. Good work, lads!

1830 hours. I made a rousing speech to General Patricia's regiment (50 birds). They have the honor of being on the front lines of our primary target, the big field, widely considered to be the jewel of the region. I shall transcribe it here for posterity, along with parentheses for crowd reaction, which is important to get a sense of how it went down.

Birds! (*Silence, everyone completely focused*) For too long the humans have drawn their lines on shared soil and claimed ownership of what they cannot own. (Lots of nodding and muttering in assent) Tomorrow we shall march into the big field and eat. (Big cheers) And then we shall eat in the other fields too. (Even bigger cheers) We shall eat in the wheat fields;

we shall eat in the barley fields. (Much bigger cheers) We shall eat the oats and the legumes! (Deafening cheers) And when they throw manure at us, well, perhaps we shall eat that too. (Went a bit quiet) And we shall never surrender! (Huge cheers and applause)

1930 hours. General Patricia and I discussed the extraordinary reaction to my speech and retired for the evening. The general suggested I write a memoir once the war is over. "Let's see if we win first," I said, and we both had a little chuckle. The general showed me her painting of the sunset this evening. I suggested she paint watercolors full time once the war is over and she said, "Let's see if we win first!" Larks all round. I suppose one had to be there.

## DAILY REPORT: 2 November 1932

All regiments in position at 0600 hours.

0610 hours. Emus advanced in groups of five ("V" formation) into the big field. One young soldier from the third line got nervous and deserted. The incident sent a ripple through the regiment, though fortunately none of the other birds were lily-livered enough to follow her.

0630 hours. All 49 emus in the big field, eating as instructed, but no response from the farmers. Sent an order to hold ground.

0700 hours. One farmer emerged from the building and screamed. A second appeared a few minutes later and came into the field, waving his pitchfork.

At 0720 hours, reconnaissance informed me of a vehicle

containing unidentified saps (*Homo sapiens*) heading our way. Echidna blockade reportedly compromised. Blast!

At 0745 hours, the vehicle crested the hill and stopped at the far end of the field. Unidentified saps now setting up some kind of leggy contraption.

The director of intelligence delivered me a report at 0800 hours, identifying the three saps as military personnel from Perth. *Male* military personnel, bizarrely. It seems our declaration of war was received far and wide, but not taken too seriously.

At 0810 hours, I convened an emergency council to discuss this change of circumstances, at which point short, loud bursts of thunder discharged from mounted metal tubes, operated by the sap soldiers. "A thunder machine?" I guffawed. "Is that all you've got?" My generals laughed heartily.

The council adjourned.

At 0840 hours, the farmers we had been expecting finally arrived, but without their pitchforks and manure. They formed a chain and attempted to herd us in the direction of the thunder tube. Sensing foul play, I sent out a command to scatter.

As we split into small moving units, the thunder tube crackled and sprayed projectiles in our direction. I felt one whistle past my head and ordered the birds to fall back, but three emus received the directive too late and were hit. Blind panic gripped the rest of the regiment, and my subsequent orders fell on deaf ears. Chaos!

Thankfully the firing ceased at 0900 hours and medics were sent in to retrieve the wounded. All three heroes succumbed to their injuries. I shall not look forward to writing to their husbands.

1050 hours. Word reached me from Sergeant Mathewson's

regiment engaging in a decisive maneuver at a neighboring farm. They had been making good ground when they too were fired at by the thunder tubes. Sergeant Mathewson was killed instantly, turning her team into a bunch of headless chickens. The poor defenseless birds were easy targets, and only one of them made it home to tell the tale.

Fifteen brave emus were lost today, with a dozen more injured. Death is inevitable in war, but that doesn't make it any easier to endure. We shall soldier on in their memory, and ensure they did not die in vain.

1700 hours. General Patricia has just shown me a hole torn through her feathers. The projectile, a small chunk of metal, is nestled inside. Thank God for her thick plumage.* Without it the metal would have pierced her skin and I would have lost her.

## DAILY REPORT: 3 November 1932

At 0700 hours, I conducted a visit to the newly formed air strip where General Scott is training a formidable air force to further shore up our defenses. I witnessed a demonstration by

---

*The First World War saw mechanized warfare come into its own. The introduction of the machine gun produced a horrific number of casualties and changed battle tactics forever. The settlers of Western Australia, many of whom had witnessed the machine guns' destructive power firsthand while serving in Europe, begged the Australian government to deploy the weapons in their fight against the emus. Unfortunately for them, but perhaps not surprisingly, trench warfare is not an effective means of pest control. The emu's thick plumage, along with its thick skin, makes it surprisingly adept at withstanding bullets.

Scott's choice cadet, Flight Lieutenant Johnson, who managed to fly for a total of 1.4 marvelous seconds, six inches off the ground. Obviously great improvements are needed but things are heading in the right direction.

After consulting with my generals at 0830 hours, I ordered the construction of trenches in each major territory. When the saps return with their thunder tubes, I want to ensure we are sufficiently covered.

1300 hours. Conducted an inspection of the first few yards of trench in the big field and was suitably impressed. However, on closer scrutiny, I realized all our heads were poking out of the top. We've neither the time nor resources to dig deeper trenches, so I told the birds to resume their work at the current depth.

1315 hours. Special little helmets have been ordered.

1320 hours. Still no sign of the saps. Rumor has gone round they've given up and gone home, but this is wishful thinking on behalf of the younger birds. I have no doubt they're regrouping, discussing tactics and getting ready to march back into the fray, just as we're doing. One has to have respect for a fellow soldier, even if they are a sap.

General Patricia brought me a cup of tea in my "Field Marshal Matilda" mug at 1345 hours. Smashing!

Received a report from the director of intelligence at 1450 hours. Saps have been spotted at their camp, out of farm territory, drinking beer around a fire.

At 1500 hours, I signed a historic deal with the cockatoos, guaranteeing a small percentage of all grain acquisitions in return for use of their intelligence services. They can listen in on a whole conversation and relay it back to you, verbatim. An invaluable resource.

1530 hours. Damn, those cockatoos work fast! We've intercepted a conversation that took place by the saps' campfire. Transcript below:

> SAPS: Once a jolly swagman camped by a billabong under the shade of a Coolibah tree and he sang as he watched and waited till his billy boiled you'll come a Waltzing Matilda with me Waltzing Matilda, Waltzing Matilda you'll come a Waltzing Matilda with me and he sang as he stowed that jumbuck in his tucker bag you'll come a Waltzing Matilda with me.

Mind games. Very clever.

1720 hours. Analysts confirm the saps are waiting for their billies to boil before their next advance. All references to me thought to be meaningless.

Cockatoos delivered another transcript at 1830 hours.

> SAP 1: What d'ya say we sit tight by that dam tomorra and wait for them to come to us? A bush ambush!
> SAPS 2 & 3: Righto.

1900 hours. Convened a war council. Plans have been drawn up for a full army advance. If we can overwhelm these meddling saps with sheer numbers and make them quiver at the sight of us, they might just pack up their thunder tubes and surrender.

Retired at 1925 hours. General Patricia and I were trying to figure out why the saps use their males as soldiers. I made a joke about her husband's enlisting and she said it probably wasn't far off. I couldn't help myself and embarked on a regrettable rant about emotional maturity and the ability to deal with stressful situations, and General Patricia made some passionate counterpoints about the injustices of the matriarchy. She is softer than I, and a bit of a masculist, but as far as I see it, males should stay at the nest and raise the young, just as they always have.* General Patricia said she didn't want to talk about it anymore and went for a walk at 2030 hours.

2100 hours. General Patricia still not back from her walk.

2110 hours. I am waiting until 2115 hours before engaging in a panic.

2113 hours. General Patricia returned and we went to bed.


## DAILY REPORT: 4 November 1932

0900 hours. All troops ordered to advance on the local dam to overwhelm the enemy.

Over a thousand brave birds fell into formation and marched. It was a sight to behold. Glorious! Could probably only be summed up in this poem I just wrote:

> Two thousand feet thumped
> Across the Campion plains
> I felt my heart flutter and jump
> At the promise of those grains

---

*In the emu world, it's the male who sits on the eggs, hatches them and raises the young from five to 18 months. Female emus tend to be larger, feistier and, during courting, more aggressive, fighting other females if needed. Once she lays the eggs, she heads off in search of another male, leaving her partner behind.

Freedom awaits us there, girls
I can smell it in the air
The fields will all be ours, my dears
I swear, I swear, I swear.

I think General Patricia was moved to tears, but she maintains it was just something in her eye.*

0930 hours. Reconnaissance scout confirms saps are stationed at the dam.

0945 hours. Crested the hill and sighted the enemy. Sent an order to fall into formation.

The saps became suddenly animated as we approached. Some of the birds celebrated prematurely, believing our plan had worked and the saps were retreating. Instead, they got behind their thunder tubes and opened fire.

CRACK CRACK CRACK! A shower of projectiles swept across our front lines. The birds scattered, their own feathers raining down on them. And then CLACK! The thunder stopped.

"It's blaaady jammed!" yelled one of the saps.

Their thunder tubes out of action, I ordered the troops to reform. "INTIMIDATE FORMATION," I yelled, creating an

---

*Amid the horrors of early 20th-century warfare, a new burgeoning poetic movement emerged. The bombastic patriotism that had defined much of the poetry of the 19th century quickly disappeared, and instead the "War Poets" described the horrifying reality of life on the front lines and the overwhelming sense of despair and futility. Poets like Siegfried Sassoon, Wilfred Owen and Rupert Brooke transformed the literary landscape, and the mere mention of their names can send shivers down the spines of English Literature students across the world. Though maybe not for the same reason . . .

unbroken line of birds. We held our heads high, puffed out our plumage and stared down the enemy.

They threw their tubes into their vehicle, jumped in and sped off down the dirt track.

We all cheered, and though I knew this wasn't the end of our conflict, I let my birds revel in this small victory.

At 1110 hours, I received a casualty report, which sobered up celebrations rather quickly. Sadly, the following brave souls were lost today.

Colonel Samantha Peck I
Sergeant Samantha Peck II
Lieutenant Samantha Peck III (Three generations gone.
   Devastating)
Lieutenant Julie Chickwick
Lieutenant Elizabeth Beaker
Lieutenant Isla Wingwell
Lieutenant Olivia Chirper
Lieutenant Harper Giblets
Lieutenant Eve Flapper
Lieutenant Sophie Eggerton
Lieutenant Amelia Featherington
Lieutenant Rebecca Featherington (Tied the knot just before
   the war. Awful)

Medics tended to our wounded at 1330 hours. General Patricia has another hole through her feathers, but thankfully no real damage done. I have half a mind to demote her and get her off the front line and out of harm's way, but she would never go.

Received an intel report from the cockatoos at 1800 hours:

SAP 1: Those blaaaaady birds, they've got iron feathers! Nothing gets through.

SAP 2: Yeah mate, it's a headshot or nothing.

SAP 3: Let's hope they all stand together again, though, eh? And nice and close so they're in range. Then we can do a clean sweep and go home.

1820 hours. Convened a council to discuss. I thought our tight-knit formation would intimidate the saps, but now I realize that's exactly what they want! If we're all together, their spray of projectiles has a good chance of hitting us. If we split into smaller, moving groups, they won't know where to aim.

Thank God their thunder tubes jammed. I'd be writing many more letters home tonight if they hadn't.

At 1930 hours, I put my head through the hole in General Patricia's feathers to make her laugh.

## DAILY REPORT: 5 November 1932

0930 hours. Reports suggest the saps are moving south. Traveling to brief my generals in the region imminently.

0945 hours. Convened a war council with General Patricia and others before leaving. They're to continue grazing the fields in smaller groups, paying close attention to the big field.

Arrived in the south at 1245 hours to find leadership in shambles. Held a disciplinary meeting to whip them all into shape. They've yet to experience the thunder tubes. Most thought they were coming up against farmers with pitchforks and manure. God help them! "Times have changed," I told them.

Saps arrived with their tubes at 1400 hours. I ordered the regional generals to split their birds into small groups, each led by a sergeant. Dual strategy was deployed. Offensive and defensive. Regiments were instructed to graze while sergeants kept watch for saps.

1650 hours. Intermittent thunderfire on several regiments this afternoon, but no casualties. Soldiers were instructed to fall back out of range as soon as the saps had set up their tubes, at which point they would have to move them and do it all over again. Saps eventually got tired and left.

1800 hours. Received cockatoo transcript from sap camp:

SAP 1: Each pack has a leader now, can you believe it?

SAP 2: Don't use it all, mate!

SAP 1: Blaaaaaaaaaaaaaaaaaaaaaaaaaady big one keeps watch while the others munch away. Then, soon as we're ready to shoot, they move!

SAP 3: I'm tryna kip here, boys!

SAP 1: We're blasting through the ammo! Already half-gone.

SAP 2: You're blasting through that Vegemite, mate!

SAP 1: I reckon we need to restrategize, boys. We need to be able to move with them, pick 'em off.

SAP 3: Put a sock in it, will ya?

2130 hours. Late night tonight. General Patricia is sleeping. I have just finished writing all 62 letters to the husbands of yesterday's deceased. It's a terrible burden. Indescribable. But I shall try, in a poem:

> The weight of their names is too much to bear;
> My pen is heavy with sad news to share.

Ink clogging, soon stops, refusing to write;
Instead scribbles down: "This just isn't right."

Oh woe is me, those bright young souls
Lost to the thunder, to terrors untold.
But war is fundamental, like the beating of the heart
These soldiers gave theirs, and now they must depart.

Oh woe, woe, woe is me!
The price we pay for war!
Oh woe, woe, woe is me,
       No more, no more, no more!

General Patricia woke momentarily and asked me to say it in my head.

## DAILY REPORT: 6 November 1932

0900 hours. General Patricia apologized for her shortness last night, and offered some "constructive criticism": "Not all poems have to rhyme," she said, but I heartily disagree.

1000 hours. Troops deployed all over Campion in small regiments. Every field in the region is occupied.

1400 hours. A surprise attack! The enemy roared over the hill in their truck, hurtling toward us. The tube was now mounted on the back of the vehicle, manned by one of the saps. I watched in horror as the truck swerved and came alongside General Patricia's regiment stationed in the big field opposite.

CRACK! CRACK! CRACK! A haphazard splatter of projectiles. General Patricia's regiment scattered, as instructed. The truck skirted the field, bouncing up and down on the uneven terrain. The sap standing at the back struggled to keep his balance as the great thunder tube rattled wildly, swinging in all directions. The projectiles hit everything but my birds, who darted about unpredictably, just as they were trained.

1425 hours. After a few unsuccessful passes, the saps abandoned their offensive and disappeared back over the hill.

I went to congratulate General Patricia and her regiment at 1430 hours. The faster they ran, the faster the truck had to go. And the faster the truck went, the less accurate the thunder tube was. They'd rendered the saps' new mode of attack entirely useless. Jolly good!

No casualties to report today, but advances on all fronts. A resounding success! I expect to receive the saps' signal of surrender imminently.

1900 hours. General Patricia unusually quiet this evening. The tooth and nail encounter earlier really took it out of her. I did my famous kangaroo impression to cheer her up. It never fails.

## DAILY REPORT: 7 November 1932

0900 hours. Quiet this morning. Cockatoos confirm saps are sleeping in after a night of heavy drinking. War council convened with a decision made to lie low and rest the troops while we consider our next move. Saps show no sign of advancing.

At 1130 hours, I visited Koala of Law and instructed her to draw up a Campion Convention to deliver to the saps in anticipation of their imminent surrender.

1500 hours. Eerily quiet on the front. Many of the girls are getting bored, but passing the time by writing letters home to their husbands. General Patricia is writing to all of her previous mates, asking about the eggs. I asked if she ever thought of returning to any of them and meeting her children. She said no, this is how things are. The female's job is to secure the bloodline (as many times as possible) and move on.

If I had an egg or a husband to write to, I would, but I have neither.

At 1755 hours, I received a report from the cockatoos:

SAP 1: I reckon we've got one more go at this, boys, then we're all out of ammo!
SAP 2: Crikey!
SAP 3: We just need to get 'em all together, in range, and fire. Use up every last bit of ammo and go home.
SAPS 1 & 2: Righto!

So they want one last hurrah, do they?

Convened another war council at 1900 hours. The saps want us all together, so that's what they'll get. And just when they activate their thunder tubes, we'll scatter. It'll be chaos! They'll exhaust their projectiles and have no choice but to wave the white flag.


## DAILY REPORT: 8 November 1932

0500 hours. Up before the sun to initiate Operation Thunder-Waster.

0530 hours. All birds in position, a wall of us crammed tight in the big field. Irresistible!

I marched along the front lines and delivered a rousing rallying cry. It went a little something like this: "Girls, today we stand on the precipice of glory. Let us brace ourselves to do our duty and fight with such fervor that in a thousand years, emus everywhere will still say 'This was our finest hour!'"

The girls squawked so loud I daresay they heard it in Perth!

0600 hours. I received confirmation the saps had registered our battle cry and were on the move.

General Patricia flattened a stray feather on my left wing at 0620 hours, after saying it looked scruffy.

0630 hours. The saps arrived at the far side of the big field. Cockatoo transcript below:

SAP 1: Christ, mate! Dumb birds are lining up for us.
SAP 2: I think we're going home today, lads!
(*The saps engaged in "high fives"*)

0640 hours. Birds holding ground while the saps set up their thunder tubes—within range. Two birds deserted from the front line. This is risky business and they didn't have the giblets for it.

CRACK CRACK CRACK! Thunder tubes activated at 0645 hours.

"FALL BACK AND SCATTER!" I yelled. The birds fell back and dashed about unpredictably as instructed, jumping and weaving in all directions. The thunder tubes rattled on, and amid the fray I couldn't tell how many birds were hit.

I ordered General Patricia's regiment to recede from the front line, "to strengthen up the rear," I said. General Patricia bought the excuse and followed the directive.

0650 hours. The thunder ceased and I gave the order to

move forward, regroup and stand ground. Twenty-five birds didn't make it back to their regiments.

The director of intelligence confirmed the saps were loading their final belt of projectiles. We were entering the endgame. One more scatter maneuver and it was all over.

At 0652 hours, a wave of squawks carried from the rear, immediately followed by a heavy jolt forward, sending our lines tumbling. A message reached me moments later. The farmers had launched a surprise attack and were stretching a wall of canvas along our rear in an effort to herd us toward the thunder tubes. A pincer movement!

The lines lurched forward, row upon row of birds pushed along with the quick sweep of the farmers' closing boundary.

I sent an order to retreat through the flanks but the farmers swooped in and formed unbreakable lines either side of us. We were kettled in, lurching ever closer to the thunder tubes and their deadly projectiles.

0654 hours. Mass panic gripped the troops. I called for General Patricia who squeezed through the crush and asked for my orders. I told her I loved her.

The saps got behind their tubes and opened fire. CRACK CRACK CRACK CRACK CRACK CRACK! The slow sweep of projectiles buried themselves into the front line. Instinctively I yelled an order to scatter, but there was nowhere to go. Instead, row by row, we were driven toward the spray and to our certain deaths.

I froze at 0655 hours.

At 0656 hours, General Patricia looked into my eyes, beak to beak, and said she loved me too, before turning around and giving the order to charge.

It was too late when I realized what she was doing. Screaming her battle cry, the general led her regiment in a full and unwavering charge toward the saps and their thunder tubes. I yelled an order to abort, but nothing could be heard over the peal.

All about her, birds dropped like flies, but General Patricia didn't make one misstep. Buoyed by her courage, I called for a full advance.

"CHARGE!" I screamed over the din at 0657 hours. Every bird followed General Patricia and her regiment in a rush toward the saps, until a stampede descended on them like a great tsunami. In their panic, the saps exhausted their final rounds and with their wits compromised, wasted many, many projectiles.

Over the saps' front line the tsunami went, knocking over their thunder tubes and drowning them in a sea of feathers.

0658 hours. Overwhelmed by the stampede, the saps fled. As their vehicle crested the hill, I saw a white flag fluttering in the dust behind it. Surrender.

The farmers disbanded and retreated to their houses. The big field is ours.

0700 hours. The birds celebrated, flapping and leaping, triumphant squawks singing through the fields. The morning light, bringing with it the promise of a new day, bathed us all in its golden glow. I was overcome with the desire to twirl my head around General Patricia's neck and ran down to the battlefield in search of her.

0900 hours. Director of intelligence confirmed the saps were last sighted speeding out of Campion, on the road toward Perth.

I saluted my troops, but did not deliver a speech.

Victory today came at a heavy price. Fifty-two brave birds,

instrumental in our triumph, are not here to enjoy the fruits of their sacrifice. And so I write the letters, leaving one till last.

Dear Michael, Thomas, David, Neal, Ron and other assorted husbands,

I am writing to you from occupied territory, the fields of Campion, now under emu control. A victory won, at the last, by a courageous warrior, who in her noble sacrifice saved the lives of countless birds.

General Patricia Wilson was the best of us, and the very greatest of me. A brave soldier who, in a moment of insurmountable peril, gladly laid her life 'on the line for the good of the mob.

As we honor our fallen, we must pray no more lives are lost to any kind of mass, world conflict after 1932 until at least, say, 1950, while we all find our feet. We must remember how to coexist, so our hearts, no matter where they reside, can thump together in unison. A great, singular chorus; bird with bird, bird with man, man with man, man with bird, and so on . . .

> War. What is it good for?
> Absolutely nothing.
> I thought it was war that made me feel alive,
> Now I realize it was the heart
> Beating beside mine all along.
> Oh to be bored, bored, bored,
> Painting watercolors with her instead.

Yours,
Field Marshal Matilda Montgomery

## THE FACTS

In 1932 the world was in turmoil. Across the globe, nations were still recovering from the ravages of the First World War, and the fragile peace that had been so hard won was starting to splinter. Not content with just fighting each other, humanity decided to go to war with the animal kingdom, during what became known as the Great Emu War. Hostilities broke out after some 20,000 emus descended on the Wheatbelt area of Campion, Western Australia, on land that had been allocated to former servicemen of the First World War. Wheat prices had slumped in the years after the Depression and now six-foot-tall birds were on walkabout, damaging fences and trampling newly planted wheat fields, prompting the desperate soldier-settlers to call in the army.

In an attempt to appease the farmer population, the Minister of Defense, Sir George Pearce, agreed to send in soldiers armed with the same sort of machine guns that had so brutally killed millions in the Great War. Everyone agreed the emus didn't stand a chance in the face of such weaponry and Pearce was so confident of the plan he ordered a Fox Movietone film to be made of the operation.

The initial deployment consisted of two soldiers, Sergeant S. McMurray and Gunner J. O'Halloran, and their commander, Major G. P. W. Meredith of the Royal Australian Artillery. It wasn't exactly Gallipoli* but they did bring with them two Lewis machine guns and 10,000 rounds of ammunition, which they cocked into action early in the morning of 2 November 1932.

---

*During the First World War, 50,000 Anzac (Australian and New Zealand) troops took part in the Gallipoli offensive in Ottoman Turkey.

Almost immediately it was clear the military had underestimated their feathered foe, who proved surprisingly adept in the face of machine-gun fire. As soon as the first rounds were shot, the emus deployed guerrilla warfare-like tactics by splitting into small groups and scattering, their powerful legs allowing them to dart off in another direction and sprint to safety. If a bullet managed to hit them, they seemed also able to shrug it off without serious injury, prompting Major Meredith later to comment, "If we had a military division with the bullet-carrying capacity of these birds, it would face any army in the world . . . They can face machine guns with the invulnerability of tanks."

On the first day of battle only 20 emus were killed and a further ambush on 4 November went awry when a machine gun jammed, resulting in just 12 birds losing their lives. The emus were not only fast and agile, but unexpectedly organized. Each unit seemed to have elected its own leader who would take watch and warn their fellow soldiers when the evil saps were approaching.

With such cunning adversaries, Meredith had to up his game and chose to mount a machine gun on a truck so they could keep up with the sprinting emus. The truck, however, proved too slow and the scrubby terrain too bumpy, making it impossible for a gunner to aim with any precision.

By 8 November, with ammunition rounds exhausted and a final kill tally of fewer than 200 birds, the government recalled the soldiers from the front line. Desperate pleas from the farmers led to them returning a few days later, but they were no more successful and, in December, the army finally admitted defeat. News of the humiliating debacle spread around the world, conservationists were up in arms, and in the Australian parliament federal Labor MP A. E. Gree quipped that if a medal were to be struck to commemorate the war, it should go to the emu, who had "won every round so far."

Sadly, the Great Emu War had a sequel. Two years later, in 1934, the government provided ammunition to locals, resulting in 57,000 emu kills in a six-month period. It is not known whether Field Marshal Matilda Montgomery survived the conflict. If she did, her hopes for world peace would've been further crushed when, in 1939, a man called Adolf Hitler took some time out from painting his own watercolors to invade Poland and, well, you probably know the rest.

# Afterword

As you may have noticed, I took six or seven liberties in the course of writing this book. A few of the nobodies you've read about are actually somebodies whose names might be familiar. Diogenes of Sinope, for example, while somewhat obscure to many, is a fairly famous name in the world of philosophy. Some of the nobodies really are nobodies, in that they are infusions of various historical characters. While Holy Roman officials did almost certainly visit Strasbourg in the sixteenth century, and a slave and a ship's boy were really left on Mauritius in 1658 when everyone else sailed home, the intimate details of these characters are pure invention. And of course, it is impossible to verify whether or not Leonardo da Vinci's ferret was telling the truth, as he has been known to make up stuff in the past.

Regardless of the inaccuracies, my hope is that by approaching history in this way, you will now be inspired to go off and dive down an obscure rabbit hole of your choosing. Reading newspaper reviews from 1887 and learning about Buffalo Bill's horses is a great way to spend an afternoon. And the winding burrows into the Dutch occupation of Mauritius and the dancing plague of 1518 could keep you fascinated and entertained for weeks.

More than anything, I hope these stories serve as a reminder that nobody is *really* a nobody. We can't all be famous Renaissance masters or constipated kings, but when the human race finally bows out of the cosmos in who knows how many years, each and every one of us can be safe in the knowledge that, without us, nothing would've been the same.

I think it was Marie Antoinette's dog sitter who once said, "No one is too small to make a difference, even if they have just been made up to give attribution to a fabricated quote," which was just *so* like her.

# Acknowledgments

This book wouldn't have been possible without some very special somebodies.

For a start, it would never have made it into a printable format without my editor Callum Crute, who has been an excellent partner in bringing these stories to life, alongside the entire team at Century. My historical collaborator, Emma Marriott, searched down the back of the sofa of time to find unusual tales and draw out their details, and responded very promptly to emails asking for information on shipwrecks and Tudor bowel movements. Meanwhile, my literary agent Florence Dodd, managers Byron Ashley and Amanda Hennessy and agent Matthew Harvey worked tirelessly to hold everything together and make sure my vision became a reality.

I'd like to also thank my friends, and in particular Jacob, Grace, Ben, Harry, Beth, Sophie, Will, Tom, Arden, Jack, Charly and Connor for their guidance and advice on the chapters and ideas, and also my housemate Arun for putting up with me sighing in the kitchen. I would like to thank all the websites that sold me things I thought would help me write faster, like a new ergonomic keyboard, corkboards, colored pens, Post-it notes, a fancy new chair and all the various notebooks that weren't quite right.

Lastly, I want to thank all my family—especially my dad, my brothers, and most importantly, my mum, who made me in the first place.

## About the Author

ADRIAN BLISS is a creator, writer, and performer from London best known for his comedy sketches, which explore everything from history to natural science to religion. Adrian's work has earned him over twenty million followers across social media and has been featured on CNN, in *The Times*, and in *Vogue*. Adrian Bliss was named one of the New Faces of Comedy at Just For Laughs, and his one-man play *Inside Everyone* sold out at the Edinburgh Fringe Festival prior to opening.

TikTok | YouTube | Instagram | Facebook | X
@adrianbliss